Django Project Blueprints

Develop stunning web application projects with the
Django framework

Asad Jibran Ahmed

BIRMINGHAM - MUMBAI

Django Project Blueprints

Copyright © 2016 Packt Publishing

First published: May 2016

Production reference: 1240516

Published by Packt Publishing Ltd.
Livery Place
35 Livery Street
Birmingham B3 2PB, UK.

ISBN 978-1-78398-542-5

www.packtpub.com

Credits

Author
Asad Jibran Ahmed

Reviewer
Jaakko Tulkki

Commissioning Editor
Julian Ursell

Acquisition Editor
Larissa Pinto

Content Development Editor
Parshva Sheth

Technical Editor
Danish Shaikh

Copy Editor
Tasneem Fatehi

Project Coordinator
Nikhil Nair

Proofreader
Safis Editing

Indexer
Mariammal Chettiyar

Production Coordinator
Arvindkumar Gupta

Cover Work
Arvindkumar Gupta

About the Author

Asad Jibran Ahmed is an experienced programmer who has worked mostly with Django-based web applications for the past 5 years. Based in Dubai, UAE, he has worked with some of the biggest web properties in the region, including *Dubizzle*, the number one classifieds platform in UAE; *Nabbesh*, one of the top freelancing platforms in the MENA region; and Just Property, a hot and rising name in the property portal space of the region.

His experience with such big names has given him a keen insight into how to design performant, stable, and user friendly web applications, all the while using programming practices that make sure that the code base is maintainable for years.

I'd like to thank my parents for all the love and support they gave me when I was playing around with computers as a child. If it had not been for their encouragement in those early years, I might not be a programmer today, and this book might not exist.

Also, to all my siblings and friends, I'd like to say thank you for putting up with it all.

About the Reviewer

Jaakko Tulkki is currently based in Madrid, Spain, where he is working as a Python developer. He has also worked in start-ups. Jaakko is currently finalizing his MSc degree in software engineering. Python is one of his favorite tools because he finds it a very productive language.

Jaakko works for Sainsbury's in Manchester, UK.

www.PacktPub.com

eBooks, discount offers, and more

Did you know that Packt offers eBook versions of every book published, with PDF and ePub files available? You can upgrade to the eBook version at www.PacktPub.com and as a print book customer, you are entitled to a discount on the eBook copy. Get in touch with us at customercare@packtpub.com for more details.

At www.PacktPub.com, you can also read a collection of free technical articles, sign up for a range of free newsletters and receive exclusive discounts and offers on Packt books and eBooks.

https://www2.packtpub.com/books/subscription/packtlib

Do you need instant solutions to your IT questions? PacktLib is Packt's online digital book library. Here, you can search, access, and read Packt's entire library of books.

Why subscribe?

- Fully searchable across every book published by Packt
- Copy and paste, print, and bookmark content
- On demand and accessible via a web browser

Table of Contents

Preface

Django is perhaps one of the most popular web development frameworks out there today. It is the framework that most Python developers reach for when they have any sizeable web application to develop.

With its proven track record of performance, scalability, and security, and its famous batteries-included approach, Django is used by some of the biggest names in the industry, including Instagram, Pinterest, and National Geographic.

This book is intended for people who have had a passing introduction to Django and a very basic idea of how to create a simple website with it. It will show you how to take your skills to the next level, developing applications as complex as e-commerce sites with lightning-fast search.

What this book covers

Chapter 1, Blueblog – A Blogging Platform, gets you started with Django and introduces the basic concepts of how to use the framework. It also introduces you to the development techniques used in the rest of the book.

Chapter 2, *Discuss – A Hacker News Clone*, walks you through creating a web application in the style of the popular Hacker News discussion forum. We look at advanced techniques to sort and rank the content of a web application based on user feedback, and then we look at spam prevention techniques.

Chapter 3, *Djagios – a Nagios Clone in Django*, covers the creation of a Nagios-like application using Django that can monitor and report on the status of remote server systems.

Chapter 4, A Car Rental App, shows you how to create a car rental application and customize the Django admin application to provide our users with a fully-featured Content Management System.

Chapter 5, Multilingual Movie DataBase, helps you create an IMDB-style web listing of movies, allowing user comments and reviews on the movies. The main focus of this chapter is allowing internationalized and localized versions of your web applications available in multiple languages.

Chapter 6, Daintree – An E-commerce site, shows you how to create an Amazon-like e-commerce website with lightning-fast search by utilizing the Elasticsearch search server software with Django.

Chapter 7, Form Mason – a Monkey of your own, helps you create a complicated and interesting web application that allows users to dynamically define web forms and then ask other people to respond to those forms, which is similar in nature to SurveyMonkey and other such sites.

Appendix, Development Environment Setup Details and Debugging Techniques, here we will look into the details of the setup, and I will explain each of the steps that we took. We will also see a technique for debugging Django applications.

What you need for this book

To create and run all the web applications that we will develop throughout the book, you will need working copies of the following software:

- The Python programming language
- pip: The package manager for installing Python packages
- virtualenv: A tool for creating isolated environments for Python packages

You can download the Python programming language for your operating system from `https://www.python.org/downloads/`. You will need Python 3 to follow the examples in this book.

You can find the instructions to install the pip package management tool at `https://pip.pypa.io/en/stable/installing/`.

You can install virtualenv by following the instructions at `https://virtualenv.pypa.io/en/latest/installation.html`.

Who this book is for

If you are a Django web developer able to build basic web applications with the framework, then this book is for you. This book will help you gain a deeper understanding of the Django web framework by guiding you through the development of six amazing web applications.

Conventions

In this book, you will find a number of text styles that distinguish between different kinds of information. Here are some examples of these styles and an explanation of their meaning.

Code words in text, database table names, folder names, filenames, file extensions, pathnames, dummy URLs, user input, and Twitter handles are shown as follows: "We can include other contexts through the use of the `include` directive."

A block of code is set as follows:

```
[default]
exten => s,1,Dial(Zap/1|30)
exten => s,2,Voicemail(u100)
exten => s,102,Voicemail(b100)
exten => i,1,Voicemail(s0)
```

When we wish to draw your attention to a particular part of a code block, the relevant lines or items are set in bold:

```
[default]
exten => s,1,Dial(Zap/1|30)
exten => s,2,Voicemail(u100)
exten => s,102,Voicemail(b100)
exten => i,1,Voicemail(s0)
```

Any command-line input or output is written as follows:

```
# cp /usr/src/asterisk-addons/configs/cdr_mysql.conf.sample
    /etc/asterisk/cdr_mysql.conf
```

New terms and **important words** are shown in bold. Words that you see on the screen, for example, in menus or dialog boxes, appear in the text like this: "Clicking the **Next** button moves you to the next screen."

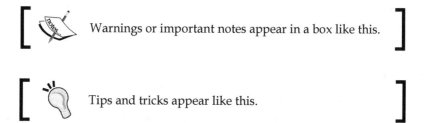

Warnings or important notes appear in a box like this.

Tips and tricks appear like this.

Reader feedback

Feedback from our readers is always welcome. Let us know what you think about this book—what you liked or disliked. Reader feedback is important for us as it helps us develop titles that you will really get the most out of.

To send us general feedback, simply e-mail feedback@packtpub.com, and mention the book's title in the subject of your message.

If there is a topic that you have expertise in and you are interested in either writing or contributing to a book, see our author guide at www.packtpub.com/authors.

Customer support

Now that you are the proud owner of a Packt book, we have a number of things to help you to get the most from your purchase.

Downloading the example code

You can download the example code files for this book from your account at http://www.packtpub.com. If you purchased this book elsewhere, you can visit http://www.packtpub.com/support and register to have the files e-mailed directly to you.

You can download the code files by following these steps:

1. Log in or register to our website using your e-mail address and password.
2. Hover the mouse pointer on the **SUPPORT** tab at the top.
3. Click on **Code Downloads & Errata**.
4. Enter the name of the book in the **Search** box.
5. Select the book for which you're looking to download the code files.
6. Choose from the drop-down menu where you purchased this book from.
7. Click on **Code Download**.

You can also download the code files by clicking on the **Code Files** button on the book's webpage at the Packt Publishing website. This page can be accessed by entering the book's name in the **Search** box. Please note that you need to be logged in to your Packt account.

Once the file is downloaded, please make sure that you unzip or extract the folder using the latest version of:

- WinRAR / 7-Zip for Windows
- Zipeg / iZip / UnRarX for Mac
- 7-Zip / PeaZip for Linux

The code bundle for the book is also hosted on GitHub at https://github.com/PacktPublishing/Django-Project-Blueprints. We also have other code bundles from our rich catalog of books and videos available at https://github.com/PacktPublishing/. Check them out!

Errata

Although we have taken every care to ensure the accuracy of our content, mistakes do happen. If you find a mistake in one of our books — maybe a mistake in the text or the code — we would be grateful if you could report this to us. By doing so, you can save other readers from frustration and help us improve subsequent versions of this book. If you find any errata, please report them by visiting http://www.packtpub.com/submit-errata, selecting your book, clicking on the **Errata Submission Form** link, and entering the details of your errata. Once your errata are verified, your submission will be accepted and the errata will be uploaded to our website or added to any list of existing errata under the Errata section of that title.

To view the previously submitted errata, go to https://www.packtpub.com/books/content/support and enter the name of the book in the search field. The required information will appear under the **Errata** section.

Piracy

Piracy of copyrighted material on the Internet is an ongoing problem across all media. At Packt, we take the protection of our copyright and licenses very seriously. If you come across any illegal copies of our works in any form on the Internet, please provide us with the location address or website name immediately so that we can pursue a remedy.

Please contact us at copyright@packtpub.com with a link to the suspected pirated material.

We appreciate your help in protecting our authors and our ability to bring you valuable content.

Questions

If you have a problem with any aspect of this book, you can contact us at questions@packtpub.com, and we will do our best to address the problem.

1
Blueblog – a Blogging Platform

We are going to start with a simple blogging platform in Django. In recent years, Django has emerged as one of the clear leaders in web frameworks. When most people decide to start using a web framework, their searches lead them to either **Ruby on Rails (RoR)** or Django. Both are mature, stable, and extensively used. It appears that the decision to use one or the other depends mostly on which programming language you're familiar with. Rubyists go with RoR, Pythonistas go with Django. In terms of features, both can be used to achieve the same results, although they have different approaches to how things are done.

One of the most popular blogging platforms these days is Medium, widely used by a number of high profile bloggers. Its popularity stems from its elegant theme, and simple-to-use interface. I'll walk you through creating a similar application in Django, with a few surprise features that most blogging platforms don't have. This will give you a taste of things to come, and show you just how versatile Django can be.

Before starting any software development project, it's a good idea to have a rough roadmap of what we would like to achieve. Here's a list of features that our blogging platform will have:

- User should be able to register an account and create their blogs
- Users should be able to tweak the settings of their blogs
- There should be simple interface for users to create and edit blog posts
- Users should be able to share their blog posts on other blogs on the platform

I know this seems like a lot of work, but Django comes with a couple of `contrib` packages that speed up our work considerably.

The contrib packages

The `contrib` packages are a part of Django that contain some very useful applications that the Django developers decided should be shipped with Django. The included applications provide an impressive set of features, including some that we'll be using in this application:

- **Admin** is a full featured CMS that can be used to manage the content of a Django site. The Admin application is an important reason for the popularity of Django. We'll use this to provide an interface for site administrators to moderate and manage the data in our application

- **Auth** provides user registration and authentication without requiring us to do any work. We'll be using this module to allow users to sign up, sign in, and manage their profiles in our application

There are a lot more goodies in the `contrib` module. I suggest you take a look at the complete list at `https://docs.djangoproject.com/en/stable/ref/contrib/#contrib-packages`.

I usually end up using at least three of the `contrib` packages in all my Django projects. They provide often-required features like user registration and management, and free you to work on the core parts of your project, providing a solid foundation to build upon.

Setting up our development environment

For this first chapter, I'll go into some details about setting up the development environment. For later chapters, I'll only be providing minimal instructions. For further details about how I setup the development environment and why, take a look at *Appendix, Development Environment Setup Details and Debugging Techniques*.

Let's start by creating the directory structure for our project, setting up the virtual environment and configuring some base Django settings that need to be set up in every project. Let's call our blogging platform BlueBlog.

Detailed explanations of the steps you're about to see are given in *Appendix, Development Environment Setup Details and Debugging Techniques*. Please refer to that if you're unsure about why we're doing something or what a particular command does.

To start a new project, you need to first open up your terminal program. In Mac OS X, it is the built-in terminal. In Linux, the terminal is named separately for each distribution, but you should not have trouble finding it; try searching your program list for the word terminal and something relevant should show up. In Windows, the terminal program is called the command line. You'll need to start the relevant program depending on your operating system.

> If you are using the Windows operating system, you will need to slightly modify the commands shown in the book. Please refer to the *Developing on Windows* section of *Appendix, Development Environment Setup Details and Debugging Techniques* for details.

Open the relevant terminal program for your operating system and start by creating the directory structure for our project; cd (ing) into the root project directory using the commands shown below:

```
> mkdir -p blueblog
> cd blueblog
```

Next let's create the virtual environment, install Django, and start our project:

```
> pyvenv blueblogEnv
> source blueblogEnv/bin/activate
> pip install django
> django-admin.py startproject blueblog src
```

With that out of the way, we're ready to start developing our blogging platform.

Database settings

Open up the settings found at $PROJECT_DIR/src/blueblog/settings.py in your favorite editor and make sure that the DATABASES settings variable matches this:

```
DATABASES = {
    'default': {
        'ENGINE': 'django.db.backends.sqlite3',
        'NAME': os.path.join(BASE_DIR, 'db.sqlite3'),
    }
}
```

In order to initialize the database file, run the following commands:

```
> cd src
> python manage.py migrate
```

Static files settings

The last step in setting up our development environment, is configuring the `staticfiles contrib` application. The staticfiles application provides a number of features that make it easy to manage the static files (css, images, JavaScript) of your projects. While our usage will be minimal, you should look at the Django documentation for staticfiles in further detail, since it is used quite heavily in most real world Django projects. You can find the documentation at `https://docs.djangoproject.com/en/stable/howto/static-files/`.

In order to set up the staticfiles application we have to configure a few settings in the `settings.py` file. First, make sure that `django.contrib.staticfiles` is added to the `INSTALLED_APPS`. Django should have done that by default.

Next, set `STATIC_URL` to whatever URL you want your static files to be served from. I usually leave this to the default value, `/static/`. This is the URL that Django will put in your templates when you use the static template tag to get the path to a static file.

A base template

Next let's setup a base template that all the other templates in our application will inherit from. I prefer to have templates that are used by more than one application of a project in a directory named templates in the project source folder. To set that up, add `os.path.join(BASE_DIR, 'templates')` to the `DIRS` array of the `TEMPLATES` config dictionary in the settings file, and then create a directory named templates in `$PROJECT_ROOT/src`. Next, using your favorite text editor, create a file named `base.html` in the new folder with the following content:

```
<html>
<head>
    <title>BlueBlog</title>
</head>
<body>
    {% block content %}
    {% endblock %}
</body>
</html>
```

Much like Python classes inheriting from other classes, Django templates can also inherit from other templates. And just like Python classes can have functions overridden by their subclasses, Django templates can also define blocks that children templates can override. Our `base.html` template provides one block for inheriting templates to override, called **content**.

The reason for using template inheritance is code reuse. We should put HTML that we want to be visible on every page of our site, such as headers, footers, copyright notices, meta tags, and so on, in the base template. Then, any template inheriting from it will automatically get all that common HTML included automatically, and we will only need to override the HTML code for the block we want to customize. You'll see this principal of creating and overriding blocks in base templates used throughout the projects in this book.

User accounts

With the database setup out of the way, let's start creating our application. If you remember, the first thing on our list of features is to allow users to register accounts on our site. As I've mentioned before, we'll be using the auth package from the Django contrib packages to provide user account features.

In order to use the auth package, we'll need to add it our `INSTALLED_APPS` list in the settings file (found at `$PROJECT_ROOT/src/blueblog/settings.py`). In the settings file, find the line defining `INSTALLED_APPS` and make sure that the string `django.contrib.auth` is part of the list. It should be by default, but for some reason if it's not there, add it manually.

You'll see that Django has included the auth package and couple of other contrib applications to the list by default. A new Django project includes these applications by default because almost all Django projects end up using these.

 If you need to add the auth application to the list, remember to use quotes to surround the application name.

We also need to make sure that the MIDDLEWARE_CLASSES list contains django. contrib.sessions.middleware.SessionMiddleware, django.contrib. auth.middleware.AuthenticationMiddleware, and django.contrib.auth. middleware.SessionAuthenticationMiddleware. These middleware classes give us access to the logged in user in our views, and also make sure that if I change the password for my account, I'm logged out from all other devices that I previously logged on to.

As you learn more about the various contrib applications and their purpose, you can start removing any that you know you won't need in your project. Now, let's add the URLs, views and templates that allow the users to register with our application.

A user accounts app

In order to create the various views, URLs, and templates related to user accounts, we'll start a new application. To do so, type the following in your command line:

```
> python manage.py startapp accounts
```

This should create a new accounts folder inside the src folder. We'll add code that deals with user accounts in files found inside this folder. To let Django know that we want to use this application in our project, add the application name (accounts) to the INSTALLED_APPS setting variable; making sure to surround it in quotes.

Account registration

The first feature we will work on is user registration. Let's start by writing the code for the registration view inside accounts/views.py. Make sure that the contents of views.py match what is shown here:

```python
from django.contrib.auth.forms import UserCreationForm
from django.core.urlresolvers import reverse
from django.views.generic import CreateView


class UserRegistrationView(CreateView):
    form_class = UserCreationForm
    template_name = 'user_registration.html'

    def get_success_url(self):
        return reverse('home')
```

I'll explain what each line of this code is doing in a bit. But first, I'd like you to get to a state where you can register a new user and see for yourself how the flow works. Next, we'll create the template for this view. In order to create the template, you first need to create a new folder called `templates` inside the `accounts` folder. The name of the folder is important, since Django automatically searches for templates in folders of that name. To create this folder, just type the following command:

```
> mkdir accounts/templates
```

Next, create a new file called `user_registration.html` inside the `templates` folder and type in the code shown below:

```
{% extends "base.html" %}

{% block content %}
<h1>Create New User</h1>
<form action="" method="post">{% csrf_token %}
    {{ form.as_p }}
    <input type="submit" value="Create Account" />
</form>
{% endblock %}
```

Finally, remove the existing code in `blueblog/urls.py` and replace it with this:

```
from django.conf.urls import include
from django.conf.urls import url
from django.contrib import admin
from django.views.generic import TemplateView
from accounts.views import UserRegistrationView

urlpatterns = [
    url(r'^admin/', include(admin.site.urls)),
    url(r'^$', TemplateView.as_view(template_name='base.html'),
name='home'),
    url(r'^new-user/$', UserRegistrationView.as_view(), name='user_
registration'),
]
```

That's all the code we need to get user registration in our project! Let's do a quick demonstration. Run the development server by typing the following command:

```
> python manage.py runserver
```

In your browser, visit `http://127.0.0.1:8000/new-user/` and you'll see a user registration form. Fill that in, and click submit. You'll be taken to a blank page on successful registration. If there are some errors the form will be shown again with the appropriate error messages. Let's verify that our new account was indeed created in our database.

For the next step, we will need to have an administrator account. The Django auth contrib application can assign permissions to user accounts. The user with the highest level of permission is called the **super user**. The super user account has free reign over the application and can perform any administrator actions. To create a super user account, run this command:

```
> python manage.py createsuperuser
```

 Since you already have the `runserver` command running in your terminal, you will need to quit it first by pressing *Ctrl + C* in the terminal. You can then run the `createsuperuser` command in the same terminal. After running the `createsuperuser` command, you'll need to start the `runserver` command again to browse the site.

If you want to keep the `runserver` command running and run the `createsuperuser` command in a new terminal window, you will need to make sure you activate the virtual environment for this application by running the same source `blueblogEnv/bin/activate` command that we ran earlier when we created our new project.

After you have created the account visit `http://127.0.0.1:8000/admin/` and log in with the admin account. You will see a link titled **Users**. Click that and you should see a list of users registered in our app. It will include the user you just created.

Congrats! In most other frameworks, getting to this point with a working user registration feature would take a lot more effort. Django, with it's batteries included approach, allows us to do the same with a minimum of effort.

Next, I'll explain what each line of code that you wrote does.

Generic views

Here's the code for the user registration view again:

```
class UserRegistrationView(CreateView):
    form_class = UserCreationForm
    template_name = 'user_registration.html'

    def get_success_url(self):
        return reverse('home')
```

Our view is pretty short for something that does such a lot of work. That's because instead of writing code from scratch to handle all the work, we use one of the most useful features of Django, generic views. Generic views are base classes included with Django that provide functionality commonly required by a lot of web apps. The power of generic views comes from the ability to customize them to a great degree with ease.

 You can read more about Django generic views in the documentation available at `https://docs.djangoproject.com/en/stable/topics/class-based-views/`.

Here, we're using the `CreateView` generic view. This generic view can display a `ModelForm` using a template and on submission can either redisplay the page with errors if the form data was invalid or call the `save` method on the form and redirect the user to a configurable URL. The `CreateView` can be configured in a number of ways.

If you want a `ModelForm` to be created automatically from some Django model, just set the `model` attribute to the `model` class, and the form will be generated automatically from the fields of the model. If you want the form only show certain fields from the model, use the `fields` attribute to list the fields you want, exactly like you'd do when using a `ModelForm`.

In our case, instead of having a `ModelForm` generated automatically, we're providing one of our own; `UserCreationForm`. We do this by setting the `form_class` attribute on the view. This form, which is part of the auth contrib app, provides the fields and a `save` method that can be used to create a new user. As we start developing more complicated applications in later chapter, you'll see that this theme of composing solutions from small reusable parts provided by Django is a common practice in Django web app development, and in my opinion is one of the best features of the framework.

Finally, we define a `get_success_url` function that does a simple reverse URL and returns the generated URL. The `CreateView` calls this function to get URL to redirect the user to when a valid form is submitted and saved successfully. To get something up and running quickly, we left out a real success page and just redirected the user to a blank page. We'll fix this later.

Template and URLs

The template, which extends the base template we created earlier simply displays the form passed to it by the `CreateView` using the `form.as_p` method, which you might have seen in the simple Django projects you may have worked on before.

The `urls.py` file is a bit more interesting. You should be familiar with most of it, the parts where we include the admin site URLs and the part where we assign our view a URL. It's the usage of `TemplateView` that I want to explain here.

Like the `CreateView`, the `TemplateView` is another generic view provided to us by Django. As the name suggests, this view can render and display a template to the user. It has a number of customization options. The most important one is `template_name`, which tells it which template to render and display to the user.

We could have created another view class that subclassed the `TemplateView`, and customized it by setting attributes and overriding functions like we did for our registration view. But I wanted to show you another method of using a generic view in Django. If you only need to customize some basic parameters of a generic view; in this case we only wanted to set the `template_name` parameter of the view, you can just pass the values as `key=value` pairs as function keyword arguments to the `as_view` method of the class when including it in the `urls.py` file. Here, we pass the template name which the view renders when the user access it's URL. Since we just needed a placeholder URL to redirect the user to, we simply use the blank `base.html` template.

This technique of customizing generic views by passing key/value pairs only makes sense when you're interested in customizing very basic attributes, like we do here. In case you want more complicated customizations, I advice you subclass the view, otherwise you will quickly get messy code that is difficult to maintain.

Login and logout

With registration out of the way, let's write code to provide users with the ability to log in and log out. To start, the user needs some way to go to the login and registration pages from any page on the site. To do this, we'll need to add header links to our template. This is the perfect opportunity to demonstrate how template inheritance can lead to much cleaner and less code in our templates.

Add the following lines right after the `body` tag in our `base.html` file:

```
{% block header %}
<ul>
    <li><a href="">Login</a></li>
    <li><a href="">Logout</a></li>
    <li><a href="{% url "user_registration"%}">Register Account</a></li>
</ul>
{% endblock %}
```

If you open the home page for our site now (at `http://127.0.0.1:8000/`), you should see that we now have three links on what was previously a blank page. It should look similar to the following screenshot:

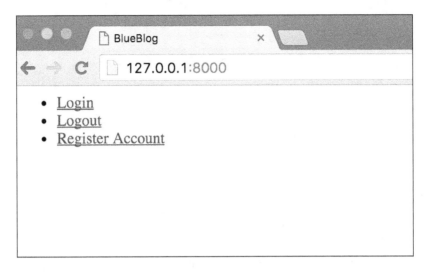

Click on the **Register Account** link. You'll see the registration form we had before, and the same three links again. Note how we only added those links to the `base.html` template. But since the user registration template extends the base template, it got those links without any effort on our part. This is where template inheritance really shines.

You might have noticed that the `href` for the login/logout links is empty. Let's start with the login part.

The login view

Let's define the URL first. In `blueblog/urls.py` import the login view from the auth app:

```
from django.contrib.auth.views import login
```

Next, add this to the `urlpatterns` list:

```
url(r'^login/$', login, {'template_name': 'login.html'},
name='login'),
```

Then create a new file inside `accounts/templates` called `login.html`. Put in the following content:

```
{% extends "base.html" %}

{% block content %}
<h1>Login</h1>
<form action="{% url "login" %}" method="post">{% csrf_token %}
    {{ form.as_p }}

    <input type="hidden" name="next" value="{{ next }}" />
    <input type="submit" value="Submit" />
</form>
{% endblock %}
```

Finally, open up `blueblog/settings.py` and add the following line to the end of the file:

```
LOGIN_REDIRECT_URL = '/'
```

Let's go over what we've done here. First, notice that instead of creating our own code to handle the login feature, we used the view provided by the auth app. We import it using `from django.contrib.auth.views import login`. Next, we associate it with the login/URL. If you remember the user registration part, we passed the template name to the home page view as a keyword parameter in the `as_view()` function. That approach is used for class-based views. For old-style view functions, we can pass a dictionary to the `url` function that is passed as keyword arguments to the view. Here, we use the template we created in `login.html`.

If you look at the documentation for the login view (`https://docs. djangoproject.com/en/stable/topics/auth/default/#django.contrib. auth.views.login`), you'll see that on successfully logging in, it redirects the user to `settings.LOGIN_REDIRECT_URL`. By default, this setting has a value of `/accounts/ profile/`. Since we don't have such a URL defined, we change the setting to point to our home page URL instead.

Next, let's define the logout view.

The logout view

In `blueblog/urls.py` import the logout view using `from django.contrib.auth. views import logout` and add the following to the `urlpatterns` list:

```
url(r'^logout/$', logout, {'next_page': '/login/'}, name='logout'),
```

And that's it. The logout view doesn't need a template; it just needs to be configured with a URL to redirect the user to after login them out. We just redirect the user back to the login page.

Navigation links

Having added the login/logout view, we need to make the links we added in our navigation menu earlier take the user to those views. Change the list of links we had in `templates/base.html` to the following:

```
<ul>
    {% if request.user.is_authenticated %}
    <li><a href="{% url "logout" %}">Logout</a></li>
    {% else %}
    <li><a href="{% url "login" %}">Login</a></li>
    <li><a href="{% url "user_registration"%}">Register Account</a>
</li>
    {% endif %}
</ul>
```

This will show the **Login and Register Account** links to the user if they aren't already logged in. If they are logged in, which we check using the `request.user.is_authenticated` function, they are only shown the **Logout** link. You can test all of these links yourself and see how little code was needed to make such a major feature of our site work. This is all possible because of the contrib applications that Django provides.

The blog

With the user registration out of the way, let's get started with the blogging side of the application. We'll create a new application for the blog, so in the console, type in the following:

```
> python manage.py startapp blog
> mkdir blog/templates
```

Add the blog application to the list of INSTALLED_APPS in our `settings.py` file. With the app created and installed, let's start with the models we'll be using.

Models

In blog/models.py, type the code shown below:

```python
from django.contrib.auth.models import User
from django.db import models


class Blog(models.Model):
    owner = models.ForeignKey(User, editable=False)
    title = models.CharField(max_length=500)

    slug = models.CharField(max_length=500, editable=False)


class BlogPost(models.Model):
    blog = models.ForeignKey(Blog)
    title = models.CharField(max_length=500)
    body = models.TextField()

    is_published = models.BooleanField(default=False)

    slug = models.SlugField(max_length=500, editable=False)
```

After typing in this code, run the following commands to create the database tables for these models:

```
> python manage.py makemigrations blog
> python manage.py migrate blog
```

This will create the database tables necessary to support our new models. The models are pretty basic. One field type that you might not have used before is the **SlugField**. A slug is a piece of text that is used to uniquely identify something. In our case, we use two slug fields to identify both our blog and our blog post. Since the fields are non-editable, we'll have to write the code to give them some values ourselves. We'll look into that later.

Creating a blog view

Let's create a view where the user can setup his blog. Let's make the form that the user will use to create a new blog. Create a new file `blog/forms.py` and enter the following:

```python
from django import forms

from blog.models import Blog


class BlogForm(forms.ModelForm):
    class Meta:
        model = Blog

        fields = [
                    'title'
                  ]
```

This creates a model form that allows edits to only the **title** field of our `Blog` model. Let's create a template and view to go along with this form.

Create a file called `blog/templates/blog_settings.html` and type in the following HTML code:

```html
{% extends "base.html" %}

{% block content %}
<h1>Blog Settings</h1>
<form action="{% url "new-blog" %}" method="post">{% csrf_token %}
    {{ form.as_p }}

    <input type="submit" value="Submit" />
</form>
{% endblock %}
```

As you may have noticed, I've used the `url` tag on the blog-settings named URL, but haven't created that URL pattern yet. We'll do that after we create the view, but just remember the name for later and make sure our URL gets the same name.

 There is no right order in which to create your view, template and URLs. It's up to you to decide whichever you are more comfortable with.

In your `blog/views.py` file, add the following code to create the view:

```python
from django.core.urlresolvers import reverse
from django.http.response import HttpResponseRedirect
from django.utils.text import slugify
from django.views.generic import CreateView

from blog.forms import BlogForm


class NewBlogView(CreateView):
    form_class = BlogForm
    template_name = 'blog_settings.html'

    def form_valid(self, form):
        blog_obj = form.save(commit=False)
        blog_obj.owner = self.request.user
        blog_obj.slug = slugify(blog_obj.title)

        blog_obj.save()
        return HttpResponseRedirect(reverse('home'))
```

Modify `blueblog/urls.py`. Add this to the top of the file `from blog.views import NewBlogView` and add this to the `urlpatterns` list:

```python
url(r'^blog/new/$', NewBlogView.as_view(), name='new-blog'),
```

As a final step, we need some way for the user to access our new view. Change the header block in `base.html` to look like this:

```html
{% block header %}
<ul>
    {% if request.user.is_authenticated %}
    <li><a href="{% url "new-blog" %}">Create New Blog</a></li>
    <li><a href="{% url "logout" %}">Logout</a></li>
    {% else %}
    <li><a href="{% url "login" %}">Login</a></li>
    <li><a href="{% url "user_registration"%}">Register Account</a></li>
    {% endif %}
</ul>
{% endblock %}
```

To test our latest feature, open up the home page at `http://127.0.0.1:8000` and click the **Create New Blog** link. It will present a form where you can enter the blog title and save your new blog. The page should look similar to the following screenshot:

Most of the code we have added is pretty basic. The interesting part is the `NewBlogView`. Let's look at how it works. First of all, notice that we subclass it from the `CreateView` generic view. The create view allows us to easily display and process a form that will create a new object of the given model. To configure it, we can either set the `model` and `fields` attribute of the view, which the create view will then use to generate a model form, or we can manually create a model form and assign it to the view, like we've done here.

We also configure the template that will be used to display the form. We then define the `form_valid` function, which the create view calls when the form is submitted with valid data. In our implementation, we call the model forms `save` method with the `commit` keyword parameter set to `False`. This tells the form to create a new object of our model with the data it was passed, but not to save the created object to the database. Then we set the owner of the new blog object to the logged in user and set its slug to a slugified version of the title entered by the user. slugify is one of the many utility functions that Django provides. Once we've modified the blog object per our requirement, we save it and return an `HttpResponseRedirect` from the `form_valid` function. This response is returned to the browser which then takes the user to the home page.

Until now, we've made do with a blank page with just a navigation bar as our home page. But it has a serious problem. Start by creating a new blog by following the link in the navigation bar. On successfully creating a new blog, we are redirected back to the home page, where we are again greeted with a link to create another blog. But this isn't the behavior we want. Ideally, our users should be limited to one blog per account.

Let's fix this. First, we'll restrict the blog creation view to only allow users to create a blog if they don't already have one. Import `HttpResponseForbidden` and the `Blog` model in `blog/views.py`:

```
from django.http.response import HttpResponseForbidden
from blog.models import Blog
```

Add a `dispatch` method to the `NewBlogView` class with the following code:

```
def dispatch(self, request, *args, **kwargs):
    user = request.user
    if Blog.objects.filter(owner=user).exists():
        return HttpResponseForbidden ('You can not create more than
one blogs per account')
    else:
        return super(NewBlogView, self).dispatch(request, *args,
**kwargs)
```

The `dispatch` method is one of the most useful methods to override on generic views. It is the first method that is called when the view URL is hit, and decides based on the request type whether to call the `get` or `post` methods on the view class to process the request. Thus, if you ever want to have some code that is run on all request types (GET, POST, HEAD, PUT, and so on), dispatch is the best method to override.

In this case, we make sure that the user doesn't already have a blog object associated with their account. If they do, we return the `Not Allowed` response by using the `HttpResponseForbidden` response class. Try it out. You shouldn't even be able to access the new blog page now if you have already created a blog before and should see an error instead.

One last thing. Try accessing the URL http://127.0.0.1:8000/blog/new/ after logging out. Notice how you'll get an AnonymousUser object is not iterable error. This is because even though you're not logged in as a registered user, the code for the view still assumes that you are. Also, you should not be able to access the new blog page without logging in first. To fix this, first put these two import lines at the top of blog/views.py:

```
from django.utils.decorators import method_decorator
from django.contrib.auth.decorators import login_required
```

Then change the definition line of the dispatch method to match the following:

```
@method_decorator(login_required)
def dispatch(self, request, *args, **kwargs):
```

If you try to access the page now without logging in first, you should see a Page not found (404) Django error page. If you look at the URL for that page, you'll see that Django is trying to serve the /accounts/login/ URL. That's the default behavior for the login_required decorator. To fix this we need to change the value of the LOGIN_ URL variable in our settings file. Put this in blueblog/settings.py:

```
LOGIN_URL = '/login/'
```

Try accessing http://localhost:8000/blog/new/ now and you will be redirected to the login page. If you put in the correct username/password combination, you will be logged in and taken to the page you were trying to access before, the **Create New Blog** page. This functionality is provided to us for free because we use the built-in login view of Django.

We'll discuss the method_decorator and the login_required decorator in later chapters. If you want more info on these now, look at their documentation in the Django docs. It does an excellent job of explaining both.

You will find the documentation for login_required at https://docs. djangoproject.com/en/stable/topics/auth/default/#the-login- required-decorator. For the method_decorator, you can look at https:// docs.djangoproject.com/en/stable/topics/class-based-views/ intro/#decorating-the-class.

The home page

It's high time that we created a proper home page for our users instead of showing a blank page with some navigation links. Also, it seems very unprofessional to show users the **Create New Blog** link when it leads to an error page. Let's fix all these issues by creating a home page view that contains a bit of intelligence. We'll put the code for our home page view in the blog application. Technically it can go anywhere, but I personally like to put such views in either the main application of the project (the blog in this case) or create a new application for such common views. In your `blog/views.py` file, import the `TemplateView` generic view `from django.views. generic import TemplateView` and put the following code for the view:

```python
class HomeView(TemplateView):
    template_name = 'home.html'

    def get_context_data(self, **kwargs):
        ctx = super(HomeView, self).get_context_data(**kwargs)

        if self.request.user.is_authenticated():
            ctx['has_blog'] = Blog.objects.filter(owner=self.request.
user).exists()

        return ctx
```

Tie this new view to the home page URL by importing it in `blueblog/urls.py` using `from blog.views import HomeView` and changing the existing root URL config from `url(r'^$', TemplateView.as_view(template_name='base.html'), name='home')`, to `url(r'^$', HomeView.as_view(), name='home')`,.

Since the `TemplateView` class is no longer required, you can remove it from the imports. You should already have a good idea of what we're doing here. The only new thing is the `TemplateView` and it's `get_context_data` method. The `TemplateView` is another one of Djangos built-in generic views. We configure it by providing a template file name and the view renders that template by passing it the dictionary returned by our `get_context_data` function as the context. Here, we are setting the `has_blog` context variable to `True` if the user has an existing blog associated with his account.

With our view done, we'll need to make a few changes to our `base.html` template and add a new `home.html` template. For the `base.html` template, change the code in the header block to match:

```html
{% block header %}
<ul>
    {% if request.user.is_authenticated %}
```

```
    {% block logged_in_nav %}{% endblock %}
    <li><a href="{% url "logout" %}">Logout</a></li>
    {% else %}
    <li><a href="{% url "login" %}">Login</a></li>
    <li><a href="{% url "user_registration"%}">Register Account</a></
li>
    {% endif %}
</ul>
{% endblock %}
```

We've removed the **Create New Blog** link and replaced it with another block called `logged_in_nav`. The idea is that each page that inherits from the base template can add navigation links here to be shown to a logged in user. Finally, create a new file called `blog/templates/home.html` and add the following code:

```
{% extends "base.html" %}

{% block logged_in_nav %}
{% if not has_blog %}
<li><a href="{% url "new-blog" %}">Create New Blog</a></li>
{% else %}
<li><a href="">Edit Blog Settings</a></li>
{% endif %}
{% endblock %}
```

Just like we discussed, the home page template overrides the `logged_in_nav` block to add a link to create a new blog if the user doesn't have an existing blog, or to edit the settings for the existing blog. You can test that all of our changes work by visiting the home page with a user that has a blog already created, and a new user without a blog. You'll see that link to create a new blog only shows up if the user hasn't already created one.

Next, let's work on the settings view.

The blog settings view

Put the code for the view in `blog/views.py`:

```
class UpdateBlogView(UpdateView):
    form_class = BlogForm
    template_name = 'blog_settings.html'
    success_url = '/'
    model = Blog

    @method_decorator(login_required)
```

```
    def dispatch(self, request, *args, **kwargs):
        return super(UpdateBlogView, self).dispatch(request, *args,
**kwargs)
```

You'll need to import `UpdateView` from `django.views.generic`. Also, update the `get_context_data` method of the `HomeView` in the same file to match this one:

```
def get_context_data(self, **kwargs):
    ctx = super(HomeView, self).get_context_data(**kwargs)

    if self.request.user.is_authenticated():
        if Blog.objects.filter(owner=self.request.user).exists():
            ctx['has_blog'] = True
            ctx['blog'] = Blog.objects.get(owner=self.request.user)
    return ctx
```

Change the `blog/templates/blog_settings.html` to look like the following:

```
{% extends "base.html" %}

{% block content %}
<h1>Blog Settings</h1>
<form action="" method="post">{% csrf_token %}
    {{ form.as_p }}

    <input type="submit" value="Submit" />
</form>
{% endblock %}
```

The only change we've done is to remove the URL we defined explicitly in the form action before. This way, the form will always submit to whatever URL it is served from. This is important as we'll see later.

Update `blog/templates/home.html` as shown in the following code:

```
{% extends "base.html" %}

{% block logged_in_nav %}
{% if not has_blog %}
<li><a href="{% url "new-blog" %}">Create New Blog</a></li>
{% else %}
<li><a href="{% url "update-blog" pk=blog.pk %}">Edit Blog Settings</
a></li>
{% endif %}
{% endblock %}
```

Finally, import the `UpdateBlogView` in `blueblog/urls.py` and add the following to the `urlpatterns`.

```
url(r'^blog/(?P<pk>\d+)/update/$', UpdateBlogView.as_view(),
name='update-blog'),
```

That's it. Visit the home page with the user you used to create the blog in the last section and this time you'll see a link to edit your blog instead of creating a new one. The interesting thing to look at here in the `UpdateView` subclass; `UpdateBlogView`. We only defined the form class, the template name, the success URL and the model to get a complete working update view. With these things configured, and our URLs set up so that the primary key of the object we want to edit is passed to our view as the keyword argument named `pk`, the `UpdateView` displays a form tied to the instance of the model we want to edit. In the home view, we add the users blog to the context and use it in the home template to generate a URL for the update view.

In the form, we needed to change the action attribute of the form so that on submit, it posted to the current page. Since we use the same template in both the create and update views, we need the form to submit to whatever URL it is rendered from. As you'll see in the upcoming projects as well, it is a common practice in Django to use the same template with similar views. And the way Django generic views are structured makes it easier to do.

Creating and editing blog posts

Let's create the views that users can use to create and edit blog posts. Let's start with creating a new blog post. We already created the model earlier, so let's start with the form and template we'll use. In `blog/forms.py`, create this form:

```
class BlogPostForm(forms.ModelForm):
    class Meta:
        model = BlogPost

        fields = [
                  'title',
                  'body'
                 ]
```

You'll need to import the `BlogPost` model as well. For the template, create a new file `blog/templates/blog_post.html`, and add the following content:

```
{% extends "base.html" %}

{% block content %}
<h1>Create New Blog Post</h1>
```

```html
<form action="" method="post">{% csrf_token %}
    {{ form.as_p }}

    <input type="submit" value="Submit" />
</form>
{% endblock %}
```

In `blog/views.py`, import the `BlogPostForm` and `BlogPost` model and then create the `NewBlogPostView`:

```python
class NewBlogPostView(CreateView):
    form_class = BlogPostForm
    template_name = 'blog_post.html'

    @method_decorator(login_required)
    def dispatch(self, request, *args, **kwargs):
        return super(NewBlogPostView, self).dispatch(request, *args,
**kwargs)

    def form_valid(self, form):
        blog_post_obj = form.save(commit=False)
        blog_post_obj.blog = Blog.objects.get(owner=self.request.user)
        blog_post_obj.slug = slugify(blog_post_obj.title)
        blog_post_obj.is_published = True

        blog_post_obj.save()

        return HttpResponseRedirect(reverse('home'))
```

In `blueblog/urls.py`, import the preceding view and add the following URL pattern:

```python
url(r'blog/post/new/$', NewBlogPostView.as_view(), name='new-blog-
post'),
```

And finally, change the homepage template `blog/template/home.html` to link to our new page:

```html
{% extends "base.html" %}

{% block logged_in_nav %}
    {% if not has_blog %}
    <li><a href="{% url "new-blog" %}">Create New Blog</a></li>
    {% else %}
    <li><a href="{% url "update-blog" pk=blog.pk %}">Edit Blog
Settings</a></li>
```

```
    <li><a href="{% url "new-blog-post" %}">Create New Blog Post</a></
li>
    {% endif %}
{% endblock %}
```

All of this code should be pretty familiar to you by now. We've used model forms and generic views to get the functionality we need, and all we needed to do was configure some stuff. We haven't written one line of code to create the relevant form fields, validate the user input, and to handle the various error and success scenarios.

You can test out our new view by using the **Create New Blog Post** link in the navigation on the home page.

Editing blog posts

As we did before with the `Blog` model, we'll create an edit view for the blog post using the same template as the create view. But first, we need to add a way for the user to see his blog posts with links to the edit page. To keep things simple, let's add this list to our home page view. In the **HomeView**, edit the `get_context_data` method to match the following:

```
def get_context_data(self, **kwargs):
    ctx = super(HomeView, self).get_context_data(**kwargs)

    if self.request.user.is_authenticated():
        if Blog.objects.filter(owner=self.request.user).exists():
            ctx['has_blog'] = True
            blog = Blog.objects.get(owner=self.request.user)

            ctx['blog'] = blog
            ctx['blog_posts'] = BlogPost.objects.filter(blog=blog)

    return ctx
```

At the end of `blog/templates/home.html`; after the `logged_in_nav` block ends, add the following code to override the content block and show the blog posts:

```
{% block content %}
<h1>Blog Posts</h1>
<ul>
    {% for post in blog_posts %}
    <li>{{ post.title }} | <a href="">Edit Post</a></li>
    {% endfor %}
</ul>
{% endblock %}
```

If you visit the home page now, you'll see a list of posts that the user has made. Let's create the functionality to edit the posts. Create the following view in `blog/views.py`:

```
class UpdateBlogPostView(UpdateView):
    form_class = BlogPostForm
    template_name = 'blog_post.html'
    success_url = '/'
    model = BlogPost

    @method_decorator(login_required)
    def dispatch(self, request, *args, **kwargs):
        return super(UpdateBlogPostView, self).dispatch(request,
*args, **kwargs)
```

Import this view into your `blueblog/urls.py` file and add the following pattern:

```
url(r'blog/post/(?P<pk>\d+)/update/$', UpdateBlogPostView.as_view(),
name='update-blog-post'),
```

Edit the list of blog posts we created earlier in the home page template to add the URL for editing a post:

```
{% for post in blog_posts %}
    <li>{{ post.title }} | <a href="{% url "update-blog-post" pk=post.
pk %}">Edit Post</a></li>
{% endfor %}
```

If you open the home page now, you'll see that you can click on the **Edit Post** link and that it takes you to the editing page for the blog post. One last thing we need to fix is the title of the edit blog post page. You may have noticed that even when editing, the title said **Create New Blog Post**. In order to fix this, replace the h1 tag inside `blog/templates/blog_post.html` with the following:

```
<h1>{% if object %}Edit{% else %}Create{% endif %} Blog Post</h1>
```

The context passed to the template by the `UpdateView` includes a variable called `object`. This is the instance that the user is currently editing. We check for the existence of this variable in the template. If we find it, we know that we're editing an existing blog post. If not, we know it's a new blog post being created. We detect this and set the title accordingly.

Viewing blog posts

To add a view to show blog posts, add the following view class to `blog/views.py`:

```
class BlogPostDetailsView(DetailView):
    model = BlogPost
    template_name = 'blog_post_details.html'
```

Remember to import `DetailView` generic view from `django.views.generic`. Next, create the `blog/templates/blog_post_details.html` template with the following code:

```
{% extends "base.html" %}

{% block content %}
<h1>{{ object.title }}</h1>
<p>{{ object.body }}</p>
{% endblock %}
```

Import the details view and add the following URL pattern to the `urls.py` file:

```
url(r'blog/post/(?P<pk>\d+)/$', BlogPostDetailsView.as_view(),
name='blog-post-details'),
```

Finally, change the list of blog posts in the home page template to link to the post details page from the post title:

```
{% for post in blog_posts %}
    <li><a href="{% url "blog-post-details" pk=post.pk %}">{{ post.
title }}</a> | <a href="{% url "update-blog-post" pk=post.pk %}">Edit
Post</a></li>
{% endfor %}
```

On the home page, the blog post titles should now link to the details page.

Multiple users

Until now, we've only been playing with a single user account and making our site work for that one user. Let's get to the exciting part and add sharing posts to other users blogs. However, once multiple users get added to the mix, there is one thing we should look at before moving forward.

Security

To demonstrate the complete lack of security in our application, let's create a new user account. Log out using the header link and register a new account. Next, log in with that user. You should end up on the home page and should not see any blog posts in the list.

Now, type in the URL `http://127.0.0.1:8000/blog/post/1/update/`. You should see the blog post we created from our first user in the edit view. Change either the title or the body of the blog post and click save. You are redirected back to the home page and it appears that the save has succeeded. Log in back to the first account and you'll see that the title of the blog post has been updated. This is a serious security breach and must be fixed, otherwise, any user can edit the blog posts for any other user without any restrictions.

The simple way in which we are able to solve this problem again demonstrates the power and simplicity of the Django framework. Add the following method to the `UpdateBlogPostView` class:

```
def get_queryset(self):
    queryset = super(UpdateBlogPostView, self).get_queryset()
    return queryset.filter(blog__owner=self.request.user)
```

That's it! Try opening `http://127.0.0.1:8000/blog/post/1/update/` again. This time instead of allowing you to edit the blog post of another user, you see a 404 page.

What this small piece of code does can be understood after looking at how the `UpdateView` generic view works. The generic view calls a number of small methods, each of which does a specific job. Here's a list of some of the methods that are defined by the `UpdateView` class:

- `get_object`
- `get_queryset`
- `get_context_object_name`
- `get_context_data`
- `get_slug_field`

The thing about having small methods like these is that in order to change the functionality of subclasses, we can override only one of these and fulfill our purpose, like we've done here. Read the Django documentation to figure out what these and many of the other methods used by the generic views do.

For our case, the `get_queryset` method, as the name suggests, gets the queryset within which the object to edit is searched for. We get the default `queryset` from the super method (which just returns a `self.model.objects.all()`) and return a version further filtered to only include blog posts owned by the currently logged in user. You should be familiar with relationship filters. If these are new to you, read the Django tutorial to familiarize yourself with the basics of filtering model querysets.

The reason you now see a 404 if you try to access someone else's blog post is that when the `CreateView` tries to get the object to edit, it receives a queryset that only includes blog posts owned by the currently logged in user. Since we're trying to edit someone else's blog post, it's not included in that queryset. Not finding the object to edit, the `CreateView` returns a 404.

Sharing blog post

The blog post sharing feature allows users to select the blog of another user they would like to share their blog posts with. This would allow users to gain more readers by sharing their content on the blogs of more popular writers, and readers would get to read more relevant content in one place instead of needing to discover more blogs.

The first step in making sharing possible is to add a field on the `BlogPost` model to indicate which blogs the post is shared with. Add this field to the `BlogPost` model in `blog/models.py`:

```
shared_to = models.ManyToManyField(Blog, related_name='shared_posts')
```

We are simply adding a basic Django many to many relationship field. If you'd like to review your knowledge of the features a many to many field provides, I advice you take a look at the Django tutorial again, specifically, the part that deals with M2M relationships.

One thing to note about the new field is that we had to specify `related_name` explicitly. As you might know, whenever you associate a model with another using any relationship field (`ForeignKey`, `OneToMany`, `ManyToMany`) Django automatically adds an attribute to the other model that allows easy access to the linked model.

Before we added the `shared_to` field, the `BlogPost` model already had a `ForeignKey` pointed at the `Blog` model. If you looked at the attributes available on the `Blog` model (using the shell), you would have found a `blogpost_set` attribute, which was a manager object that allowed access to `BlogPost` models that referenced that `Blog`. If we try to add the `ManyToMany` field without a `related_name`, Django would complain because the new relationship would also try to add a reverse relationship, also called `blogpost_set`. Because of this we need to give the reverse relationship another name.

After defining the M2M relationship, you can now access blog posts shared with a blog model by using the `shared_posts` attributes `all()` method on the `Blog` model. We'll see an example of that later.

After defining the new field, run the following commands to migrate your DB to create the new relationship:

```
> python manage.py makemigrations blog
```

```
> python manage.py migrate blog
```

Next, let's create the view that allows the user to select a blog to share their post with. **Add** this to `blog/views.py`:

```python
class ShareBlogPostView(TemplateView):
    template_name = 'share_blog_post.html'

    @method_decorator(login_required)
    def dispatch(self, request, *args, **kwargs):
        return super(ShareBlogPostView, self).dispatch(request, *args,
**kwargs)

    def get_context_data(self, pk, **kwargs):
        blog_post = BlogPost.objects.get(pk=pk)
        currently_shared_with = blog_post.shared_to.all()
        currently_shared_with_ids = map(lambda x: x.pk, currently_
shared_with)
        exclude_from_can_share_list = [blog_post.blog.pk] +
list(currently_shared_with_ids)

        can_be_shared_with = Blog.objects.exclude(pk__in=exclude_from_
can_share_list)

        return {
            'post': blog_post,
            'is_shared_with': currently_shared_with,
            'can_be_shared_with': can_be_shared_with
        }
```

This view is a subclass of the template view. You should have a pretty good idea of how it works by now. The important bit to look at here is the code inside the `get_context_data` method. First, we get the blog post object using the `id` passed in the keyword arguments gathered from the parsed URL pattern. Next, we get a list of all blog objects this post has been shared with. We do this because we don't want to confuse the user by allowing sharing to a blog that the post is already shared with.

The next line of code uses the Python built-in `map` method on the queryset of the blogs the post is shared with. `map` is one of the most useful methods when working with any kind of lists (or list-like objects) in Python. It takes as it's first argument a function that takes a single argument and returns one argument, and a list as it's second argument. `map` then calls the given function on each element in the input list and gathers the results in a final list that is returned. Here, we use a `lambda` to extract the ID of the blog objects that this post is already shared with.

Finally, we can get the list of blog objects that this post can be shared with. We use the `exclude` method to not include the blog objects the post is already shared with. We pass this to the template in the context. Next, let's take a look at the template that you need to create in `blog/templates/share_blog_post.html`:

```
{% extends "base.html" %}

{% block content %}
{% if can_be_shared_with %}
<h2>Share {{ post.title }}</h2>
<ul>
    {% for blog in can_be_shared_with %}
    <li><a href="{% url "share-post-with-blog" post_pk=post.pk blog_
pk=blog.pk %}">{{ blog.title }}</a></li>
    {% endfor %}
</ul>
{% endif %}

{% if is_shared_with %}
<h2>Stop sharing with:</h2>
<ul>
    {% for blog in is_shared_with %}
    <li><a href="{% url "stop-sharing-post-with-blog" post_pk=post.pk
blog_pk=blog.pk %}">{{ blog.title }}</a></li>
    {% endfor %}
</ul>
{% endif %}
{% endblock %}
```

There's nothing special in this template. Let's move on to the two URLs and views that this refers to, since without those we can't render this template. First, let's look at `SharepostWithBlog`, which you need to create in `blog/views.py`. You will need to add this import line to the top of the file as well:

```
from django.views.generic import View
```

The code for the view is this:

```
class SharePostWithBlog(View):
    @method_decorator(login_required)
    def dispatch(self, request, *args, **kwargs):
        return super(SharePostWithBlog, self).dispatch(request, *args,
**kwargs)

    def get(self, request, post_pk, blog_pk):
        blog_post = BlogPost.objects.get(pk=post_pk)
        if blog_post.blog.owner != request.user:
            return HttpResponseForbidden('You can only share posts
that you created')

        blog = Blog.objects.get(pk=blog_pk)
        blog_post.shared_to.add(blog)

        return HttpResponseRedirect(reverse('home'))
```

Import this into `blueblog/urls.py` and add it with the following URL pattern:

```
url(r'blog/post/(?P<pk>\d+)/share/$', SharePostWithBlog.as_view(),
name='share-blog-post-with-blog'),
```

Unlike all our previous views, this view doesn't fit nicely into any of the generic views that Django provides. But Django has a base generic view that makes our life easier than creating a function that handles the request.

The `View` generic view is used whenever you need something completely custom to handle a request. Like all generic views, it has a dispatch method that you can override to intercept a request before any further processing is done. Here, we make sure that the user is logged in before allowing them to proceed.

In a `View` subclass, you create methods with the same name as the request types you want to handle. Here, we create a `get` method as we only care about handling GET requests. The `View` class takes care of calling our method when the correct request method is used by the client. In our get method, we're doing a basic check to see if the user owns the blog post. If they do, we add the blog to the `shared_to` ManyToMany relationship of the `BlogPost` model.

The last view we need to create is one to allow the user to remove a blog post they have already shared. The code for that is shown here:

```
class StopSharingPostWithBlog(View):
    @method_decorator(login_required)
    def dispatch(self, request, *args, **kwargs):
```

```
        return super(StopSharingPostWithBlog, self).dispatch(request,
*args, **kwargs)

    def get(self, request, post_pk, blog_pk):
        blog_post = BlogPost.objects.get(pk=post_pk)
        if blog_post.blog.owner != request.user:
            return HttpResponseForbidden('You can only stop sharing
posts that you created')

        blog = Blog.objects.get(pk=blog_pk)
        blog_post.shared_to.remove(blog)

        return HttpResponseRedirect(reverse('home'))
```

Like the `SharePostWithBlog` view, this one subclasses the `View` generic view. The code is almost exactly the same as the previous view. The only difference is that in the previous view we used `blog_post.shared_to.add`, whereas in this view we use the `blog_post.shared_to.remove` method.

Finally, import these two views into `blueblog/urls.py` and add the following patterns:

```
url(r'blog/post/(?P<post_pk>\d+)/share/to/(?P<blog_pk>\d+)/$',
SharePostWithBlog.as_view(), name='share-post-with-blog'),
    url(r'blog/post/(?P<post_pk>\d+)/stop/share/to/(?P<blog_pk>\
d+)/$', StopSharingPostWithBlog.as_view(), name='stop-sharing-post-
with-blog'),
```

In order to show a link to the share this post page, edit the `home.html` template to change the entire code inside the `content` block to this:

```
{% if blog_posts %}
<h2>Blog Posts</h2>
<ul>
    {% for post in blog_posts %}
    <li>
        <a href="{% url "blog-post-details" pk=post.pk %}">{{ post.
title }}</a> |
        <a href="{% url "update-blog-post" pk=post.pk %}">Edit Post</
a> |
        <a href="{% url "share-blog-post" pk=post.pk %}">Share Post</
a>
    </li>
    {% endfor %}
</ul>
{% endif %}
```

And that's it. Now when you visit the home page, each blog post should have a **Share Post** link next to it. When you click it, you'll see a second page with links to share the blog post on other user blogs. Clicking the link should share your post and also show a corresponding remove link on the same page. Of course, in order to test this, you should create a second user account and add a blog using that account.

One last thing we should do is modify the `get_context_data` method of the **HomeView** to also include shared posts in the blog post list:

```python
def get_context_data(self, **kwargs):
    ctx = super(HomeView, self).get_context_data(**kwargs)

    if self.request.user.is_authenticated():
            if Blog.objects.filter(owner=self.request.user).exists():
            ctx['has_blog'] = True
            blog = Blog.objects.get(owner=self.request.user)

            ctx['blog'] = blog
            ctx['blog_posts'] = BlogPost.objects.filter(blog=blog)
            ctx['shared_posts'] = blog.shared_posts.all()

    return ctx
```

Add this to the bottom of the `content` block inside the `blog/templates/home.html` template:

```html
{% if shared_posts %}
<h2>Shared Blog Posts</h2>
<ul>
    {% for post in shared_posts %}
    <li>
        <a href="{% url "blog-post-details" pk=post.pk %}">{{ post.
title }}</a>
    </li>
    {% endfor %}
</ul>
{% endif %}
{% endblock %}
```

And that's it, our first application is complete! If you open the home page now, you should see a **Share Post** link next to each blog post. Clicking this should open up another page where you can select which blog to share this post with. To test it you should create another blog with the other account we created earlier when we were looking at the security of our application. Once you have another blog configured, your share blog post page should look similar to this:

Clicking the title of the other blog should share the post and take you back to the home page. If you click the **Share Post** link again on the same post, you should now see a heading saying **Stop sharing with**, and the name of the blog you shared this post with.

If you log in to the other account now, you should see that the post is now shared there, and is listed under the **Shared Blog Posts** section.

Summary

In this chapter, we've seen how to start our application and set it up properly so that we can develop things rapidly. We've looked at using template inheritance to achieve code reuse and give our site common elements such as navigation bars. Here's a list of topics we have covered so far:

- Basic project layout and setup with sqlite3 database
- Simple Django form and model form usage
- Django contrib apps
- Using `django.contrib.auth` to add user registration and authentication to an application
- Template inheritance
- Generic views for editing and displaying database objects
- Database migrations

We'll use the lessons we've learned here throughout the rest of the chapters in this book.

2
Discuss – a Hacker News Clone

In this chapter, we'll be creating a web app similar to Hacker News or Reddit, where users can share and discuss links to web content. We'll call the application *Discuss*. To keep things simple, we'll be emulating the minimalistic look of Hacker News, which is text only and has a very simple interface. Reddit, on the other hand, is much more visually rich and has a lot of extra features that we won't be adding to our site.

Here's an outline of what we'll be covering in this chapter:

- Allowing users to submit their own content
- Allowing users to vote on content submitted by other users
- Ranking the user-submitted content based on simple algorithms
- Preventing spammers from abusing our site using captchas

Chapter code packs

If you have developed a few Django applications, you'll probably know that for most applications, a lot of the code and configurations that you do when starting out is the same. You set up the database in the same way, maybe changing the **Database (DB)** name and user/pass pairs, you set up your media, static URL, and root paths, and then you add user authentication using the built-in `auth contrib` application and the provided views, only creating minimal templates that are good enough to get the job done in the start.

Walking you through the basic setup at the start of every chapter would be very boring—both for you to read and for me to write. Instead, I've provided what I call **Code Packs**. These are `zip` files that contain the Django application already set up so that we can jump straight to the interesting parts of the code instead of having to go through the tedious setup process again and again.

Don't worry, I won't skip any new Django features that we haven't looked at yet. Each code pack contains code that has already been explained to you in previous chapters. For instance, the code pack for this chapter contains a Django application that has the user registration, login, and logout views, templates, and URLs already set up. This is the stuff that we have already looked at in detail in the previous chapter.

To use these code packs, you will need to download them, unzip them in the project root folder, and create a virtual environment for them. Then, you'll need to run the following command to have Django installed in your new virtual environment:

```
> pip install django
```

```
> python manage.py migrate
```

Once you've done all these steps, you'll be ready to start working on the fun parts of the application. For all the following chapters, I've given you the link to the code pack and I assume that you have already extracted and set up a virtual environment for it.

 If you are not sure how to use the code packs, there is `Readme.txt` in each ZIP file. You should read this to figure out how to get started using the code pack.

Requirements

For any complex application, it is always a good idea to know what features we need to work on before we jump into coding. Let's look at what we want to create in this chapter.

We want to have a Django-based link sharing and discussion site like Hacker News. The site should have user accounts, allow users to share links, have a page where these links are listed in some defined order, and allow users to vote and comment on those links.

Additionally, we'd like to have safeguards against spammers and malicious users who would degrade the content quality of our site if left unchecked.

In a list form, here are the features that we want our application to provide:

- User registration and authentication (already provided in the code pack)
- Link submission by users
- Voting on links submitted by other users
- Commenting on the submissions and replying to comments by other users
- An algorithm to rank the submitted links in some defined order that depends on a number of factors including the votes for that link, number of comments, and age of the submission
- A way to disallow spammers from creating scripts that can automatically flood our site with submissions

Starting out

By now you should have the application ready to test if you've followed the instructions given at the start of the chapter. Let's see what it looks like at the moment. Start the application by running the following command in your terminal from the application folder. You'll need to make sure that your virtual environment is activated before you can run this command:

```
> python manage.py runserver
```

Open http://127.0.0.1:8000 in your browser and you should see the following basic page:

As you can see, we have links for **Login** and **Create New Account**. You should go ahead and create a new account. Log in with this account and you'll see the two links replaced with a **Logout** link. This is the basic application setup that we'll use moving forward. You should make sure that you are able to use the application at this point, as all further development will be built on top of this.

Link submission

Let's look at what features we want to be related with link submissions. This is just a part of the features list that we saw at the start of the chapter:

- Link submission by users
- Voting on links submitted by other users
- Commenting on the submissions and replying to comments by other users

Let's think about what models we'll need to implement this. First, we need a model to hold information about a single submission, such as the title, URL, who submitted the link, and at what time. Next, we need a way to track votes on submissions by users. This can be implemented by a ManyToMany field from the submission model to the User model. This way, whenever a user votes for a submission, we just add them to the set of related objects and remove them if they decide to take back their vote.

Commenting as a feature is separate from link submissions because it can be implemented as a separate model that links to the submission model with ForeignKey. We'll look at commenting in the next section. For now, we'll concentrate on link submissions.

To start out, let's create a new application in our project for link submission-related features. Run the following command in your CLI:

```
> python manage.py startapp links
```

Then, add our newly created app to the INSTALLED_APPS settings variable. Now we're ready to write code.

Let's start with the models. Here's the code for Link model. This code should be in links/models.py:

```
from django.contrib.auth.models import User
from django.db import models


class Link(models.Model):
    title = models.CharField(max_length=100)
```

```
    url = models.URLField()

    submitted_by = models.ForeignKey(User)
    upvotes = models.ManyToManyField(User, related_name='votes')

    submitted_on = models.DateTimeField(auto_now_add=True,
editable=False)
```

Note that we had to set `related_name` for the `upvotes` field. If we hadn't done this, we would get an error from Django when we try to run our application. Django would have complained about having two relationships to the `User` model from the `Link` model, both trying to create a reverse relationship named `link`. To fix this, we explicitly named the reverse relationship from the `User` model to the `Link` model via the `upvotes` field. The `User` model should now have an attribute called `votes`, which can be used to get a list of submissions that the user has voted on.

Once you've saved this code, you'll need to make and run migrations in order for Django to create database tables for the new model. To do so, type the following commands:

> **python manage.py makemigrations**

> **python manage.py migrate**

Next, let's work on the templates and views. We'll customize the generic `CreateView` that we've seen in the previous chapter for the view. Put this code in `links/views.py`:

```
from django.contrib.auth.decorators import login_required
from django.core.urlresolvers import reverse
from django.http.response import HttpResponseRedirect
from django.utils.decorators import method_decorator
from django.views.generic import CreateView

from links.models import Link


class NewSubmissionView(CreateView):
    model = Link
    fields = (
        'title', 'url'
    )

    template_name = 'new_submission.html'

    @method_decorator(login_required)
    def dispatch(self, *args, **kwargs):
```

```
        return super(NewSubmissionView, self).dispatch(*args,
    **kwargs)

    def form_valid(self, form):
        new_link = form.save(commit=False)
        new_link.submitted_by = self.request.user
        new_link.save()

        self.object = new_link
        return HttpResponseRedirect(self.get_success_url())

    def get_success_url(self):
        return reverse('home')
```

This should look familiar to the `CreateView` subclasses that we have already created
in the previous chapter. However, look closer! This time, we don't define a custom
form class. Instead, we just point to the model—`Link` in this case—and `CreateView`
automagically creates a model form for us. This is the power of built-in Django
generic views. They give you multiple options to get what you want, depending on
how much customization you need to do.

We define the `model` and `fields` attributes. The `model` attribute is self-explanatory.
The `fields` attribute has the same meaning here as it has in a `ModelForm` subclass.
It tells Django which fields we want to be made editable. In our `link` model, the title
and submission URL are the only two fields that we want the user to control, so we
put these in the fields list.

Another important thing to look at here is the `form_valid` function. Note that it
doesn't have any calls to `super`. Unlike our previous code, where we always called
the parent class method for methods that we had overridden, we do no such thing
here. That's because `form_valid` of `CreateView` calls the `save()` method of the
form. This will try to save the new link object without giving us the chance to set its
`submitted_by` field. As the `submitted_by` field is required and can't be `null`, the
object won't be saved and we'll have to deal with a database exception.

So instead, we chose to not call the `form_valid` method on the parent class and
wrote the code for it ourselves. To do so, I needed to know what the base method
did. So I looked up the documentation for it at `https://docs.djangoproject.com/
en/1.9/ref/class-based-views/mixins-editing/#django.views.generic.
edit.ModelFormMixin.form_valid`:

> *"Saves the form instance, sets the current object for the view, and redirects to
> get_success_url()."*

If you look at our code for the `form_valid` function, you will see that we do exactly the same thing. If you're ever faced with a similar situation, the Django documentation is the best resource to clear things up. It has some of the best documentation that I have ever encountered in any of the open source projects that I have used.

Finally, we need the template and URL configuration for the link submission feature. Create a new folder called `templates` in the `links` directory and save this code in a file called `new_submission.html`:

```
{% extends "base.html" %}

{% block content %}
    <h1>New Submission</h1>
    <form action="" method="post">{% csrf_token %}
        {{ form.as_p }}
        <input type="submit" value="Submit" />
    </form>
{% endblock %}
```

In `discuss/urls.py`, import the new view:

```
from links.views import NewSubmissionView
```

Create a new URL configuration for this view:

```
url(r'^new-submission/$', NewSubmissionView.as_view(), name='new-submission'),
```

That's it. All the code that we need to get a basic link submission process up is written. However, to be able to test it out, we'll need to give the user some way of accessing this new view. The navigation bar in our `base.html` template seems like a good place to put the link in for this. Change the code for the `nav` HTML tag in `base.html` in the `templates` directory in the project root to match the following code:

```
<nav>
    <ul>
        {% if request.user.is_authenticated %}
        <li><a href="{% url "new-submission" %}">Submit New Link</a></li>
        <li><a href="{% url "logout" %}">Logout</a></li>
        {% else %}
        <li><a href="{% url "login" %}">Login</a></li>
        <li><a href="{% url "user-registration"%}">Create New Account</a></li>
        {% endif %}
    </ul>
</nav>
```

To test it out, run the development server and open the home page. You'll see a **Submit New Link** option in the navigation menu on the top. Click on it and you'll see a page similar to the following one. Fill in the data and click on submit. If the data that you've filled in doesn't have any errors, you should be redirected to the home page.

While this works, this isn't the best user experience. Redirecting the user to the home page without giving them any feedback on whether their link was submitted is not good. Let's fix this next. We'll create a details page for the submissions and if the user was successful in submitting a new link, we'll take them to the details page.

Let's start with the view. We'll use the `DetailView` generic view provided by Django. In your `links/views.py` file, import `DetailView`:

```
from django.views.generic import DetailView
```

Subclass it for our submission detail view:

```
class SubmissionDetailView(DetailView):
    model = Link
    template_name = 'submission_detail.html'
```

Create the `submission_detail.html` template in the `links/templates` directory and put in the following Django template code:

```
{% extends "base.html" %}

{% block content %}
```

```
    <h1><a href="{{ object.url }}" target="_blank">{{ object.title
}}</a></h1>
    <p>submitted by: <b>{{ object.submitted_by.username }}</b></p>
    <p>submitted on: <b>{{ object.submitted_on }}</b></p>
{% endblock %}
```

Configure the URL for this view in `discuss/urls.py` by first importing it:

```
from links.views import SubmissionDetailView
```

Then, add a URL pattern for it to the `urlpatterns` list:

```
url(r'^submission/(?P<pk>\d+)/$', SubmissionDetailView.as_view(),
name='submission-detail'),
```

Finally, we'll need to edit the `NewSubmissionView get_success_url` method to redirect the user to our new detail view on successfully creating a new submission:

```
def get_success_url(self):
    return reverse('submission-detail', kwargs={'pk': self.object.pk})
```

That's it. Now when you create a new submission, you should see the following detail page for your new submission:

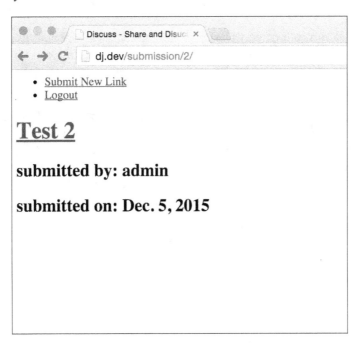

Now that link submission is done, let's look at implementing the comments feature.

Comments

We want our logged in users to be able to comment on submissions. We'd also like users to reply to comments by other users. To achieve this, our `comment` model needs to be able to track the submission it was made on and also have a link to its parent comment (if it was made in reply to some other user's comment).

If you have ever used forums on the Internet, the way our comments section works should seem familiar. One complaint that I've always had with all these forums is that they allow this hierarchy of comments to go on forever. Then you end up with 10-level deep comments that extend off the screen:

```
Comment  1
    Comment  2
        Comment  3
            Comment  4
                Comment  5
                    Comment  6
                        Comment  7
                            Comment  8
                                Comment  9
                                    Comment  10
```

While there are a number of ways to solve this, the simplest probably is to cut off nested replies beyond a certain level. In our case, no comments can be replies to `Comment  2`. Instead, they must all be in reply to `Comment  1` or the parent submission. This will make the implementation easier as we'll see later.

From our discussion so far, we know that our comment model will need foreign keys to our submission models and also to itself in order to refer to parent comments. This self reference, or a recursive relationship as Django documentation calls it, is something that I have used maybe once in the five years (and more) I have been creating web apps in Django. It's not something that is needed very often but sometimes it results in elegant solutions, like the one you'll see here.

To keep things simple, we'll first implement commenting on link submissions and later add code to handle replying to comments. Let's start with the model. Add the following to `links/models.py`:

```python
class Comment(models.Model):
    body = models.TextField()

    commented_on = models.ForeignKey(Link)
```

```
    in_reply_to = models.ForeignKey('self', null=True)

    commented_by = models.ForeignKey(User)
    created_on = models.DateTimeField(auto_now_add=True,
editable=False)
```

The `in_reply_to` field here is the recursive foreign key that allows us to create a hierarchy of comments and replies to them. As you can see, creating a recursive foreign key is achieved by giving the model name `self` instead of the model name like you would usually do with a normal foreign key.

Create and run the migrations to add this model to our database:

```
> python manage.py makemigrations
```

```
> python manage.py migrate
```

Next, let's think about the view and template. As we're only implementing commenting on submissions for now, it makes sense that the form to create a new comment also be visible on the submission details page. Let's create the form first. Create a new `links/forms.py` file and add the following code:

```
from django import forms

from links.models import Comment


class CommentModelForm(forms.ModelForm):
    link_pk = forms.IntegerField(widget=forms.HiddenInput)

    class Meta:
        model = Comment
        fields = ('body',)
```

We will just create a simple model form for the `Comment` model and add one extra field that we'll use to keep track of which link the comment needs to be associated with. To make the form available to our submission details template, import the form in `links/views.py` by adding the following to the top of the file:

```
from links.forms import CommentModelForm
```

We'll also add code to show comments for a submission on the details page now. So we need to import the `Comment` model in the views file. Right after the line importing the form, add another line of code importing the model:

```
from links.models import Comment
```

To be able to display the comments associated with a submission and the form to create a new submission, we'll need to make these two things available in the template context of the submission details page. To do so, add a `get_context_data` method to `SubmissionDetailView`:

```
def get_context_data(self, **kwargs):
    ctx = super(SubmissionDetailView, self).get_context_data(**kwargs)

    submission_comments = Comment.objects.filter(commented_on=self.
object)
    ctx['comments'] = submission_comments

    ctx['comment_form'] = CommentModelForm(initial={'link_pk': self.
object.pk})

    return ctx
```

We'll look at the initial attribute that we are passing to `CommentModelForm` in a while. We'll also need to create a view where the new comment form is submitted. Here's the code that you'll need to add it to `links/views.py`:

```
class NewCommentView(CreateView):
    form_class = CommentModelForm
    http_method_names = ('post',)
    template_name = 'comment.html'

    @method_decorator(login_required)
    def dispatch(self, *args, **kwargs):
        return super(NewCommentView, self).dispatch(*args, **kwargs)

    def form_valid(self, form):
        parent_link = Link.objects.get(pk=form.cleaned_data['link_
pk'])

        new_comment = form.save(commit=False)
        new_comment.commented_on = parent_link
        new_comment.commented_by = self.request.user

        new_comment.save()

        return HttpResponseRedirect(reverse('submission-detail',
kwargs={'pk': parent_link.pk}))

    def get_initial(self):
```

```
        initial_data = super(NewCommentView, self).get_initial()
        initial_data['link_pk'] = self.request.GET['link_pk']

    def get_context_data(self, **kwargs):
        ctx = super(NewCommentView, self).get_context_data(**kwargs)
        ctx['submission'] = Link.objects.get(pk=self.request.
GET['link_pk'])

        return ctx
```

Even though we show the form on the submission detail page, in case the user inputs incorrect data when submitting the form, such as pressing the submit button with an empty body, we need a template that can show the form again along with the errors. Create the `comment.html` template in `links/templates`:

```
{% extends "base.html" %}

{% block content %}
    <h1>New Comment</h1>
    <p>
        <b>You are commenting on</b>
        <a href{% url 'submission-detail' pk=submission.pk %}">{{
submission.title }}</a>
    </p>

    <form action="" method="post">{% csrf_token %}
        {{ form.as_p }}
        <input type="submit" value="Post Comment" />
    </form>
{% endblock %}
```

You should already know what most of the code for the `CreateView` subclass does. One thing that is new is the `get_inital` method. We'll look at it in detail later. For now, let's get the comments feature up and running.

Let's add our new view to `discuss/urls.py`. First, import the view:

```
from links.views import NewCommentView
```

Then, add it to the URL patterns:

```
url(r'new-comment/$', NewCommentView.as_view(), name='new-comment'),
```

Finally, change `links/templates/submission_detail.html` to the following:

```
{% extends "base.html" %}

{% block content %}
    <h1><a href="{{ object.url }}" target="_blank">{{ object.title
}}</a></h1>
    <p>submitted by: <b>{{ object.submitted_by.username }}</b></p>
    <p>submitted on: <b>{{ object.submitted_on }}</b></p>

    <p>
        <b>New Comment</b>
        <form action="{% url "new-comment" %}?link_pk={{ object.pk }}"
method="post">{% csrf_token %}
            {{ comment_form.as_p }}
            <input type="submit" value="Comment" />
        </form>
    </p>

    <p>
        <b>Comments</b>
        <ul>
            {% for comment in comments %}
            <li>{{ comment.body }}</li>
            {% endfor %}
        </ul>
    </p>
{% endblock %}
```

If you noticed the form action URL in our template, you'll see that we have added the `link_pk` GET parameter to it. If you refer back to the code that you wrote for `NewCommentView`, you'll see that we use this parameter value in the `get_context_data` and `get_inital` functions to get the `Link` object that the user is commenting on.

> I'm saving describing what the `get_initial` method does until the next section when we get to adding replies to comments.

Let's look at what we've made till now. Start the application using the `runserver` command, open the home page in your browser, and then log in. As we don't yet have any way to access old submissions, we'll need to create a new submission. Do that and you'll see the new detail page. It should look similar to the following screenshot:

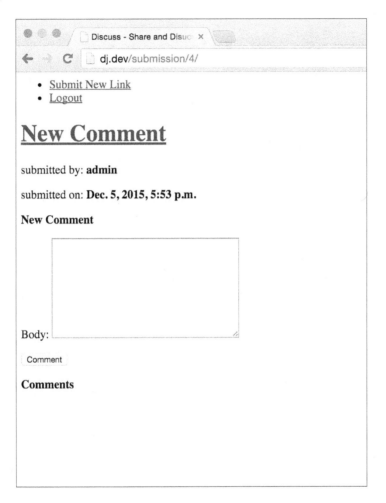

Add a comment and it should appear on the same page. Here's a screenshot with a few comments added:

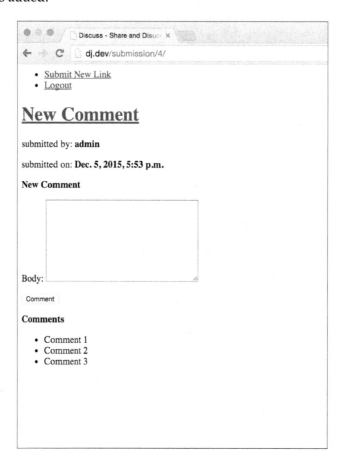

If you leave the body empty and press the **Comment** button, you should see the comment template that you created earlier with an error message:

With basic commenting on submission working, let's look at how we'll implement replying to comments. As we've already seen, our comment model has a field to indicate that it was made in reply to another comment. So all we have to do in order to store a comment as a reply to another comment is correctly set the in_reply_to field. Let's first modify our model form for the Comment model to accept in addition to a link_pk, a parent_comment_pk as well to indicate which (if any) comment is the new comment a reply to. Add this field to CommentModelForm right after the link_pk field:

```
parent_comment_pk = forms.IntegerField(widget=forms.HiddenInput,
required=False)
```

Now we need a place to show a form to the user to post his reply. We could show one form per comment on the submission details page, but that would end up making the page look very cluttered for any submission with more than a few comments. In a real-world project, we'd probably use JavaScript to generate a form dynamically when the user clicks on the reply link next to a comment and submits this. However, right now we are more focused on the Django backend and thus we'll come up with another way that doesn't involve a lot of frontend work.

A third way, which we'll be using here, is to have a little link next to each comment that takes the user to a separate page where they can record their reply. Here's the view for that page. Put this in `links/views.py`:

```python
class NewCommentReplyView(CreateView):
    form_class = CommentModelForm
    template_name = 'comment_reply.html'

    @method_decorator(login_required)
    def dispatch(self, *args, **kwargs):
        return super(NewCommentReplyView, self).dispatch(*args,
**kwargs)

    def get_context_data(self, **kwargs):
        ctx = super(NewCommentReplyView, self).get_context_
data(**kwargs)
        ctx['parent_comment'] = Comment.objects.get(pk=self.request.
GET['parent_comment_pk'])

        return ctx

    def get_initial(self):
        initial_data = super(NewCommentReplyView, self).get_initial()

        link_pk = self.request.GET['link_pk']
        initial_data['link_pk'] = link_pk

        parent_comment_pk = self.request.GET['parent_comment_pk']
        initial_data['parent_comment_pk'] = parent_comment_pk

        return initial_data

    def form_valid(self, form):
        parent_link = Link.objects.get(pk=form.cleaned_data['link_
pk'])
```

```
        parent_comment = Comment.objects.get(pk=form.cleaned_
data['parent_comment_pk'])

        new_comment = form.save(commit=False)
        new_comment.commented_on = parent_link
        new_comment.in_reply_to = parent_comment
        new_comment.commented_by = self.request.user

        new_comment.save()

        return HttpResponseRedirect(reverse('submission-detail',
kwargs={'pk': parent_link.pk}))
```

By now, having used it multiple times, you should be comfortable with `CreateView`. The only new part here is the `get_initial` method, which we also used in `NewCommentView` previously. In Django, each form can have some initial data. This is data that is shown when the form is **Unbound**. The boundness of a form is an important concept. It took me a while to wrap my head around it, but it is quite simple. In Django, a form has essentially two functions. It can be displayed in the HTML code for a web page or it can validate some data.

A form is bound if you passed in some data for it to validate when you initialized an instance of the form class. Let's say you have a `form` class called `SomeForm` with two fields, name and city. Say you initialize an object of the form without any data:

```
form = SomeForm()
```

You have created an unbound instance of the form. The form doesn't have any data associated with it and so can't validate anything. However, it can still be displayed on a web page by calling `{{ form.as_p }}` in the template (provided it was passed to the template via the context). It will render as a form with two empty fields: `name` and `city`.

Now let's say you pass in some data when initializing the form:

```
form = SomeForm({'name': 'Jibran', 'city': 'Dubai'})
```

This creates a bound instance of the form. You can call `is_valid()` on this form object and it will validate the passed data. You can also render the form in an HTML template, just like before. However, this time, it will render the form with both the fields having the values that you passed here. If, for some reason, the values that you passed didn't validate (for example, if you left the value for the city field empty), the form will display the appropriate error message next to the field with the invalid data.

This is the concept of bound and unbound forms. Now let's look at what the initial data in a form is for. You can pass initial data to a form when initializing an instance by passing it in the initial keyword parameter:

```
form = SomeForm(initial={'name': 'Jibran'})
```

The form is still unbound as you did not pass in the data attribute (which is the first non-keyword argument to the constructor) but if you render it now, the name field will have the value 'Jibran' while the city field will still be empty.

The confusion that I faced when I first learned of the initial data was why it was required. I could just pass the same data dictionary as the data parameter and the form would still only receive a value for one field. The problem with this is that when you initialize a form with some data, it will automatically try to validate that data. Assuming that the city field is a required field, if you then try to render the form in a web page, it will display an error next to the city field saying that this is a required field. The initial data parameter allows you to supply values for form fields without triggering validation on that data.

In our case, `CreateView` calls the `get_initial` method to get the dictionary to use it as the initial data for the form. We use the submission ID and parent comment ID that we will pass in the URL parameters to create the initial values for the `link_pk` and `parent_comment_pk` form fields. This way, when our form is rendered on the HTML web page, it will already have values for these two fields. Looking at the `form_valid` method, we then extract these two values from the form's `cleaned_data` attribute and use it to get the submission and parent comment to associate the reply with.

The `get_context_data` method just adds the parent comment object to the context. We use it in the template to tell the user which comment they are replying to. Let's look at the template, which you need to create in `links/templates/comment_reply.html`:

```
{% extends "base.html" %}

{% block content %}
    <h1>Reply to comment</h1>
    <p>
        <b>You are replying to:</b>
        <i>{{ parent_comment.body }}</i>
    </p>

    <form action="" method="post">{% csrf_token %}
```

```
        {{ form.as_p }}
        <input type="submit" value="Submit Reply" />
    </form>
{% endblock %}
```

Nothing fancy here. Note how we use the `parent_comment` object that we passed in the `get_context_data` method of the view. It's good UI practice to make sure that the user is always given relevant information about the action that they are about to take.

Import our new view in `discuss/urls.py`:

```
from links.views import NewCommentReplyView
```

Add this pattern to the URL patterns list:

```
url(r'new-comment-reply/$', NewCommentReplyView.as_view(), name='new-comment-reply'),
```

Lastly, we need to give the user a link to get to this page. As we discussed before, we'll be putting a link called **Reply** next to each comment on the submission detail page. To do so, note the following line in `links/templates/submission_detail.html`:

```
<li>{{ comment.body }}</li>
```

Change it to the following:

```
<li>{{ comment.body }} (<a href="{% url "new-comment-reply" %}?link_pk={{ object.pk }}&parent_comment_pk={{ comment.pk }}">Reply</a>)</li>
```

Note how we pass in the submission ID and parent comment ID using GET params when creating the URL. We did this with the comment form on the submission page as well. This is a common technique you'll use a lot when creating Django apps. These are the same URL parameters that we used in the comment reply view to populate the initial data for the form and access the parent comment object.

Let's try it out. Click on **Reply** on one of the comments on the submission detail page. If you've closed the old submission details page, you can create a new submission and add some comments to it. By clicking on the `Reply` link, you'll see a new page with a form for the comment body. Enter some text here and click on the `Submit` button. Remember the text that you entered. We'll be looking for this next in the upcoming few steps. In my testing, I entered **Reply to Comment 1**. Let's see what our submission details page looks with our new reply comment:

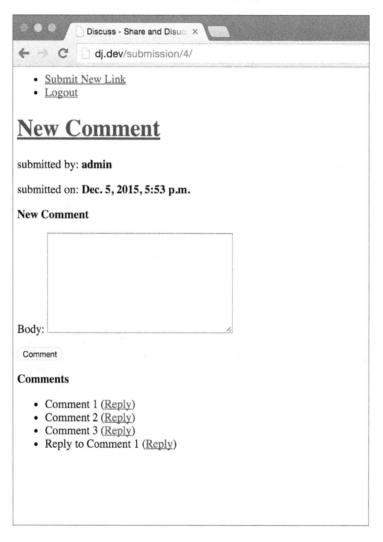

It seems like it worked. However, if you look closely, you'll notice that the reply we made (in my case, the **Reply to Comment 1** text) is shown at the end of the comments list. It should be shown after **Comment 1** and ideally indented a bit to the right as well to indicate the hierarchy. Let's fix this. First, in the `get_context_data` method of `SubmissionDetailView` in the `links/views.py` file, note this line:

```
submission_comments = Comment.objects.filter(commented_on=self.object)
```

Change it to the following:

```
submission_comments = Comment.objects.filter(commented_on=self.object,
in_reply_to__isnull=True)
```

What we've done here is include only the comments that don't have a parent comment. We do this by getting only comments that have the `in_reply_to` field set to NULL. If you save this change and refresh the submission detail page, you'll notice that your reply comment will be gone. Let's bring it back. Modify `link/templates/submission_detail.html` and change the paragraph that shows the comments (the one with the `for` loop over the comments list) to match the following:

```html
<p>
    <b>Comments</b>
    <ul>
        {% for comment in comments %}
        <li>
            {{ comment.body }} (<a href="{% url "new-comment-reply"
%}?link_pk={{ object.pk }}&parent_comment_pk={{ comment.pk }}">Reply</
a>)
            {% if comment.comment_set.exists %}
            <ul>
                {% for reply in comment.comment_set.all %}
                <li>{{ reply.body }}</li>
                {% endfor %}
            </ul>
            {% endif %}
        </li>
        {% endfor %}
    </ul>
</p>
```

The new part here is between the `if` tag. First, we use the reverse relationship that is created by the foreign key to itself to see if this comment has any other comments pointing to it. We know that the only comments pointing to this comment would be replies to this comment. If there are, we then create a new list and print the body for each of the replies. As we've already decided that we only allow replies to the first level of comments, we don't create any links to let users reply to the replies. Once you've save these changes, let's see what our submission details page looks now:

That's more like it! We now have a complete link submission and commenting system. Awesome! Let's move on to the other features now.

Voting

We need to allow users to vote on submissions. To keep things simple, we'll only allow upvotes. A user can indicate that they like a submission. There is no way to indicate disapproval. This keeps the code and UI simple. We also want to ensure that one user can upvote a submission only once and they can remove their upvotes if they change their minds or upvoted a submission by mistake.

If you take another look at the Link model, you'll see we already have an upvotes field, which is a **Machine to machine (M2M)** with the User model. This is the only database entry we'll need to allow and keep track of upvotes by users. In order to upvote a submission, users will click on a link next to the submission. Until now, we were able to make do without a page to list all submissions. It's a good idea to create one now so that we can access and upvote the various submissions. We can't keep creating new submissions every time we want to test something.

First, create this view in links/views.py. Remember to import TemplateView from django.views.generic first:

```python
class HomeView(TemplateView):
    template_name = 'home.html'

    def get_context_data(self, **kwargs):
        ctx = super(HomeView, self).get_context_data(**kwargs)
        ctx['submissions'] = Link.objects.all()

        return ctx
```

Next, change the template at template/home.html to the following:

```html
{% extends "base.html" %}

{% block content %}
    <h1>Welcome to Discuss</h1>
    <h2>Submissions</h2>
    <ul>
        {% for submission in submissions %}
        <li>
            <a href="{{ submission.url }}" target="_blank">{{ submission.title }}</a>
            <i><a href="{% url "submission-detail" pk=submission.pk %}">Comments</a></i>
        </li>
        {% endfor %}
    </ul>
{% endblock %}
```

Import our new `HomeView` at the top of `discuss/urls.py` and note the home URL configuration in `discuss/urls.py`:

```
url(r'^$', TemplateView.as_view(template_name='home.html'),
name='home'),
```

Change the preceding code to this:

```
url(r'^$', HomeView.as_view(), name='home'),
```

Finally, let's provide our users with a handy link to the home page in the navigation bar. In the `base.html` template (in the `templates` directory in the project root), add this as the first list element of the navigation list outside of the user authentication if condition:

```
<li><a href="{% url "home" %}">Home</a></li>
```

That's it. There's nothing new in this code. It's pretty easy to understand and you should have a clear idea of what's happening here by now. Let's look at the end result. If you now open the home page of our app by browsing to `http://127.0.0.1:8000` in your browser, you should see something similar to the following screenshot. Of course, your page will not be the same as this as you will have added your own test content:

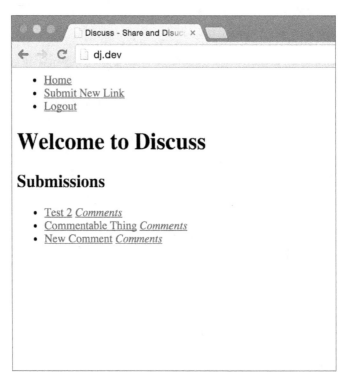

You'll see a list of submissions. If you click on any, you'll have a new tab open with the link for that submission. You'll also see a **Comments** link next to each submission. Clicking on this takes you to the submission detail page.

Let's talk a bit about how we're going to implement the upvoting feature. The M2M `upvotes` field that we created in the `Link` model should give you a hint. Whenever a user `upvotes` a submission, we add them to this relationship. As an M2M relationship ensures that if we add the same object multiple times it doesn't create a new record, we easily ensure that one user can vote on a submission only once.

Let's create a view that adds the logged in user to the upvoters list of a submission and then takes them back to the home page. We'll also add a link to each submission on the home page that lets the user upvote the submission with this new view.

In `links/views.py`, import the `View` generic view class from `django.views.generic`, and then create this view:

```
class UpvoteSubmissionView(View):
    def get(self, request, link_pk, **kwargs):
        link = Link.objects.get(pk=link_pk)
        link.upvotes.add(request.user)

        return HttpResponseRedirect(reverse('home'))
```

Next, import this new view in `discuss/urls.py` and add it to the URL patterns :

```
url(r'^upvote/(?P<link_pk>\d+)/$', UpvoteSubmissionView.as_view(),
name='upvote-submission'),
```

In `templates/home.html`, add the **Upvote** link above the submission title link:

```
<a href="{% url "upvote-submission" link_pk=submission.pk %}">Upvote</
a>
```

Open up the home page and you'll see an **Upvote** link next to each submission title. Clicking on the link should bring you back to the home page. It should look similar to the following screenshot:

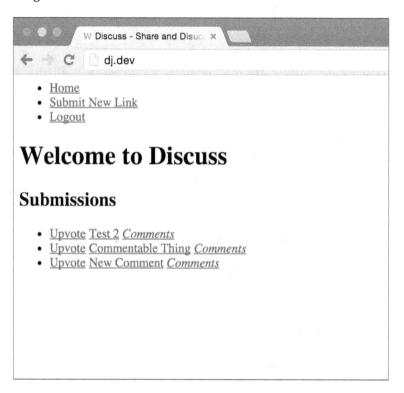

If you upvote a link, it immediately brings you back to the home page without any indication that your upvote was recorded. The fix for this is simple. Change the Upvote link HTML line that you just added to the home page template to the following:

```
{% if request.user in submission.upvotes.all %}
  Upvoted
{% else %}
  <a href="{% url "upvote-submission" link_pk=submission.pk
%}">Upvote</a>
{% endif %}
```

If you open up the home page again, you'll see a simple **Upvoted** text next to submissions that you've already upvoted instead of the link that you saw before. We should also allow the user to remove his upvote from a submission. First, create a new view for this in `links/views.py`:

```
class RemoveUpvoteFromSubmissionView(View):
    def get(self, request, link_pk, **kwargs):
        link = Link.objects.get(pk=link_pk)
        link.upvotes.remove(request.user)

        return HttpResponseRedirect(reverse('home'))
```

This is almost the same as the view we created to record a new upvote. The only difference is that here we use the remove method of the related manager. Next, we'll need to add this to the URLs file at `discuss/urls.py`. Import our new view here and add the following URL configuration:

```
url(r'^upvote/(?P<link_pk>\d+)/remove/$',
RemoveUpvoteFromSubmissionView.as_view(), name='remove-upvote'),
```

Finally, let's change the **Upvoted** label that we added to the home page before to be a link to remove the upvote. In your `templates/home.html` file, note these lines:

```
{% if request.user in submission.upvotes.all %}
  Upvoted
{% else %}
```

Change them to the following:

```
{% if request.user in submission.upvotes.all %}
  <a href="{% url "remove-upvote" link_pk=submission.pk %}">Remove
Upvote</a>
    {% else %}
```

That's it! Now when you visit the home page, you'll see the **Remove Upvote** link for all the submissions that you have already upvoted. By clicking on the link, you'll be redirected back to the home page with your upvote removed. You should see the **Upvote** link for that submission again as you can upvote it again.

Ranking submission

The next feature on our list is ranking the submissions using an intelligent algorithm. Let's take a look at what our feature description requires:

 An algorithm to rank the submitted links in some defined order that depends on a number of factors including the votes for that link, the number of comments and the age of the submission

We have all this information in our database. We need to create an algorithm that will use all these pieces of information to give each submission a rank. Then, we'll just sort the submission using this ranking and show them in the sorted order. To keep things simple, let's use the following algorithm:

```
rank = number of votes + number of comments - number of days since
submission
```

Seems simple enough, except for maybe the number of days since submission calculations. However, the `datetime` module in the Python standard library makes this a breeze for us. In Python, if you subtract two `datetime` objects, you get a `timedelta` object. This object represents the time difference between the two `datetime` objects. It has an attribute called `days` that—as is obvious by the name—holds the number of days between the two dates. We'll subtract the date that we get from `datetime.datetime.now()` from the `submitted_on` field of the submission and use the `days` attribute of the resulting `timedelta` object.

Let's plug this algorithm into our home view so that our submissions are listed by their ranks. Change `HomeView` in `links/views.py` to match the following code:

```
class HomeView(TemplateView):
    template_name = 'home.html'

    def get_context_data(self, **kwargs):
        ctx = super(HomeView, self).get_context_data(**kwargs)

        now = timezone.now()
        submissions = Link.objects.all()
        for submission in submissions:
            num_votes = submission.upvotes.count()
            num_comments = submission.comment_set.count()

            date_diff = now - submission.submitted_on
```

```
        number_of_days_since_submission = date_diff.days

        submission.rank = num_votes + num_comments - number_of_
days_since_submission

        sorted_submissions = sorted(submissions, key=lambda x: x.rank,
reverse=True)
        ctx['submissions'] = sorted_submissions

        return ctx
```

You will also need to import the `timezone` module from Django utilities using the following:

```
from django.utils import timezone
```

This is needed because Django uses something called `timezone` aware `datetimes`. For more details on this, read the Django documentation for `timezone` awareness at `https://docs.djangoproject.com/en/stable/topics/i18n/timezones/#naive-and-aware-datetime-objects`.

This new code might look a bit complicated but trust me, it's pretty simple. Let's look at it one line at a time. The first thing we do is get the current date time using the `timezone.now()` function. Next, we get all the submissions that we want to show on the home page and start looping over them.

In the loop, we first calculate the number of votes and comments on the submission using the `count()` method that you have seen before on Django `querysets`. The only different thing here is that we use it on the queryset returned by the `RelatedManager` object for the many-to-many upvotes field and the reverse relationship to the comments model.

As explained before, we then calculate the number of days since the submission was submitted to our site using the Python date arithmetic. Finally, we calculate and assign the rank for the submission to the object.

After the loop ends, each of our `Link` objects has a rank attribute that holds the final ranking for it. We then use the Python built-in `sorted` function to sort this list. When you're working with lists, which is quite often in Python and Django, the sorted function is something you will end up using many times. You should familiarize yourself with its syntax and features by reading the documentation at `https://docs.python.org/3/library/functions.html#sorted`. Trust me, it's well worth the time to read this documentation slowly and understand it completely. I have used the `sorted` built-in function more times than I can remember. It's indispensable.

Finally, we assign the sorted submissions list to the `submissions` context variable. As we are already using this variable in the home page template, we do not need to change anything else beyond `HomeView`. If you open the home page now, you'll see that the sorting order of the submissions has changed and now reflects our new algorithm.

This is a good place to reflect upon the benefits of the modularity provided by the Model-View-Template architecture used by Django. As you can see, we added quite a significant feature, but we never had to change the URLs or templates for the home page. As these are individual modules, we only changed the view code and everything else still worked with our new and improved sorting order.

Spam protection

The last feature that we want to have in our application is spam protection. We want users to be able to post content on our site, but we want to prevent abuse by spammers. Spamming, as you probably know, refers to malicious Internet users posting inappropriate or irrelevant content to a site. Often, spammers use scripts created specifically to target sites that allow user-submitted content, such as our web app. While we can't stop spammers easily from submitting spam content to our site manually, we can make sure that they are not able to use scripts to generate a lot of spam with just a click of the mouse. Usually, if spammers can't use their scripts on websites, they move on to easier targets.

The important concept that I want you to learn from this feature isn't how to implement spam protection. That's something you need to decide based on the requirements of your own project. What I'll be showing here is how to use open source Django applications created by other developers to add features to your own Django projects. This is an important concept that you should be familiar with. Most of the time, if you're looking for ways to solve an issue while developing your web app, a search of the Internet turns up a number of open source applications that were developed by other programmers to solve the same issue. You get applications solving all sizes of issues — from the smallest providing features such as a new type of form field (for example, a calendar form field that uses a JavaScript calendar) to large applications providing complete Django-based forums that you can integrate with your Django website easily and provide users with an easy-to-use and good-looking forum.

We'll be using the `ReCaptcha` service from Google to provide us with a mechanism to stop spammers. You can learn more about the service at `https://www.google.com/recaptcha`. You will also need to register for an account here and create an API key. It will ask for a label, which I set to **Discuss Django Blueprints**, and a domain, which I set to `127.0.0.1`. The `owners` field should have your e-mail address there. Once you submit this form, you'll be presented with a screen that shows you your public and private keys. Keep this page open as we'll use these values in a bit.

Next, we need to find a Django application that allows us to use the ReCaptcha service. A Google search led me to `https://github.com/praekelt/django-recaptcha`. It seems like a well-maintained and simple solution to our problem. In order to use it, we first have to install it in our virtual environment. On your command line, make sure that you have the virtual environment active. Then, install this package using the following `pip` command:

```
> pip install django-recaptcha
```

This will install the package. Next, add `captcha` to the list of `INSTALLED_APPS` in your `discuss/settings.py` file. Also, add the `RECAPTCHA_PUBLIC_KEY` and `RECAPTCHA_PRIVATE_KEY` variables to the settings file. Set their values to the appropriate keys that you were given on the Google ReCaptcha API keys page that I asked you to keep open before. **Site Key** is the public key and **Secret Key** is the private key. Finally, in your `settings.py` file, set the following variable:

```
NOCAPTCHA = True
```

The setup is ready. We're ready to use `ReCaptcha` in our forms. For demonstration, I'll only add it to the comment form that you can see on the submission detail page. Open up `links/forms.py` and add this import to the top:

```
from captcha.fields import ReCaptchaField
```

Then, add this field to `CommentModelForm`:

```
captcha = ReCaptchaField()
```

That's it! You have successfully added Google `ReCaptcha` to your website! Let's try it out. Open up the details page for any submission and now, right below the body field that we had previously for the comment, you'll see the Google `ReCaptcha` box as well:

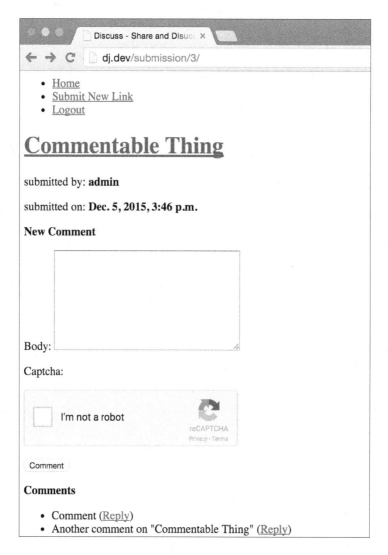

Now, if you submit the form without selecting the **I am not a robot checkbox**, you'll be taken to the comment form page with an error message saying that the captcha field is required. You won't be able to submit your comment until you select this box.

There are two takeaways from adding the ReCaptcha to our site. Firstly, notice how easy it was for us to add a relatively complicated feature using the open source code contributed by another programmer. Secondly, notice how—because of the modularity that Django provides and the separation between the template and code—all we had to do to include the ReCaptcha widget was add it to the form. We didn't even need to change the view code or template. It all worked.

Summary

This was a pretty interesting chapter. You learned a lot more about the built-in generic view provided by Django and looked in detail into ModelForms and how we could customize them. We figured out some benefits of the modular MVC pattern that Django follows and third-party open source Django applications and how we can include them in our projects.

You also learned a great deal about how to pass data to our forms even when they are placed on separate pages and how to create a form that is displayed on two pages (the comment form) while making sure that the data is synchronized between both.

All in all, the application that we ended up creating was both fun to program and a complete product.

3
Djagios – a Nagios Clone in Django

In this chapter, we'll be creating a server status monitoring solution similar to **Nagios**. It is understandable if you have never heard of Nagios as it is not something that comes up in day-to-day conversations between web developers. In a nutshell, Nagios can tell you the status of your servers (which can be in the thousands) in one screen. You can configure alerts based on conditions, for example, if some critical server becomes unresponsive, so that you can be on top of problems before your users start to notice any service degradation. Nagios is an amazing piece of software that is used by millions of organizations around the world.

Our goal in this chapter is to create something similar, albeit very simple. Our Nagios clone, creatively named **Djagios**, will allow users to set up monitoring for simple stats from their servers. We will allow the monitoring of the following:

- System load
- Disk usage

We will also be developing a web page where this data will be shown to the user in a nice tabular format. The user will also see an overview of how their servers are doing, and if any alerts are active on those systems.

Here are some of the things that we will be looking at in this chapter:

- What Django management commands are and how to create a custom one
- Using the Django shell to test out small pieces of code quickly
- Complicated validation of Django Model fields
- Slightly more complicated uses of the built-in generic views
- Creating an API endpoint to accept data from external sources
- Securing these API endpoints with simple shared secret keys
- Testing API endpoints using simple tools

Code pack

This chapter's code pack has a basic Django application setup with a SQLite database already configured. However, there isn't much code in the code pack because this chapter did not require user accounts or any other pre-existing setup. You can unzip the code pack, create a new virtual environment, activate it, and run the following commands from within the code folder to get up and running:

```
> pip install django
> python manage.py migrate
```

Requirements

Let's talk a bit about what we want from our end product before we start writing up some code. As mentioned before, we're looking to create a server monitoring solution. What exactly will it do? How can we implement the required functionality?

As our inspiration for Djagios is Nagios, let's look at how Nagios works. While Nagios is a huge application with understandably complex programming, it is in the end a client-server application. The server, which is just another computer, contains the Nagios installation. The clients, which are the systems that you want to monitor, run small plugin scripts that gather data and push it to the server. The server takes these data points and, based on how it's configured, sends out alerts if required. It also stores these data points and can show them in a simple tabular layout, giving you an instant overview of all the computer systems in your infrastructure.

We'll be creating something similar. Our server will be a Django application that will accept data points using an HTTP endpoint. The application will also include a web page where all these data points will be shown next to the client they came from. Our clients will be simple shell scripts that upload the data to our server.

For the rest of the chapter, I will call the Django application, the **server**, and the systems that you want to monitor, the **node**. These are common terms used in many other projects that you will encounter in your programming career and they often mean similar things in those other projects.

Instead of developing all of these things at once, we'll take an incremental approach. We'll first create the models to store our data points. Next, instead of moving directly to creating the HTTP endpoint to accept the data points and client-side plugin scripts, we'll take a simpler approach and come up with a way to generate some fake data to test. An finally, we will create the web page to show our users the latest status of the client nodes and the triggered alerts.

With fake data to test, we can be confident that our status page and alerting system are working correctly. We can then move forward to the next step, which will be creating the HTTP endpoint to gather data points from clients and client-side plugin scripts.

In real-world projects, this incremental approach to building software systems is often the best way to complete projects. Create simple features and test them extensively to make sure that they work. Once you are confident of their correctness, add more functionality and repeat the testing phase. This way is analogous to how a tall building is constructed. If you are confident that the foundation is strong, you can build one floor at a time without worrying if the whole thing will fall down on your head.

The model

What information should we record for the data points? We definitely need the name of the node that is sending the data. We also need to record the time at which we got the data point so that we can figure out the latest status of the node. Of course, we need to know the type and value of the data point. The type of the data point is simply the name of the quantity that we are measuring, such as CPU usage, memory usage, uptime, and so on.

For now, I think these are all the things that we need to measure:

- Node name
- Date and time
- Type
- Value

While thinking about which fields we needed in our model, I thought of another approach. It involved having a different model for each data point type, so we could have Django models named `SystemLoad`, `MemoryUsage`, `DiskUsage`, `Uptime`, and so on. However, once I thought about it further, I figured out that doing so would be very restrictive as now we'd need to define a new model every time we wanted to measure something new. Having the type of the data point as another field in our model gives us a lot of flexibility in terms of recording new types of information.

As you'll see later on, there are pros and cons to both approaches.

Let's start a new Django application in our project. In your command line, type the following, making sure that your virtual environment is activated and that you are in the project folder:

```
> python manage.py startapp data_collector
```

Add this new app to the list of `INSTALLED_APPS` in `djagios/settings.py`, and then add our data point model to `data_collector/models.py`:

```python
class DataPoint(models.Model):
    node_name = models.CharField(max_length=250)
    datetime = models.DateTimeField(auto_now_add=True)

    data_type = models.CharField(max_length=100)
    data_value = models.FloatField()
```

Save the file and then run migrations to add it to our database:

```
> python manage.py makemigrations data_collector
```
```
> python manage.py migrate
```

While the model is pretty simple, there is one thing you should be aware of. To keep things simple, I made the decision to store only numeric values; hence, the `data_value` field is of the `FloatField` type. If this were a real-world project, you would have a set of requirements that would dictate if you could make the same compromise. You might have to record text values as well, for instance, the status of some service you might be running. For Djagios, we are OK with numeric values only as all the stats that we want to measure are just numbers.

Fake data generation

Before moving on to the next step, which is creating the status page, we should come up with a way to generate some fake data. This will help us while creating the status page and debug any issues that we encounter along the way. Without any data, we could spend time creating the perfect status page, only to find out later when we add data that some aspect of it, such as the design or data layout scheme, won't work.

Django management commands

Django has a very useful feature called management commands. It allows us to create Python scripts that can interact with the rest of the Django app code we write, including our models.

The reason we can't just write a simple Python script that imports our models is that Django, like all web frameworks, has many dependencies and requires a complex setup to make sure that every thing is configured properly before we can use its features. For example, accessing the database depends on Django knowing where the settings file is because it contains the configuration for the database. Without knowing how to read the database, you can't query the models.

Let's conduct a little test. Make sure that your virtual environment is activated and that you are in the project directory. Next, start up the Python shell by typing the following:

```
> python
```

This will start a new Python interactive shell where you can type Python statements and have them executed immediately. You'll know that you are in a Python shell because your prompt will change to >>>. Now, let's try importing our DataPoint model in this shell:

```
>>> from data_collector.models import DataPoint
```

Press *Enter* and you might be surprised by the huge error message that is printed. Don't worry, you don't need to read all of it. The most important part is the last line. It will be similar to this (though not exactly as it might change slightly between different Django versions):

```
django.core.exceptions.ImproperlyConfigured: Requested setting
DEFAULT_INDEX_TABLESPACE, but settings are not configured. You must
either define the environment variable DJANGO_SETTINGS_MODULE or call
settings.configure() before accessing settings.
```

It looks intimidating, but let's look at it in parts. The first part before the colon : is the exception name. Here, Django raised the `ImproperlyConfigured` exception. Then there is a sentence telling you that some setting was requested, but settings are not yet configured. The last sentence is a helpful message about how to fix this.

While you can take the steps that are listed in the error message and get your scripts to run outside of Django, using a management command is almost always the best option. With a management command, you don't need to set up Django manually. It's done for you automatically before your script is run and you can avoid having to worry about setting environment variables such as `DJANGO_SETTINGS_MODULE` or calling `settings.configure()`.

To create a new management command, we first have to create two new Python modules to hold our command script. Type the following in your command line from the project root directory:

```
> mkdir -p data_collector/management/commands
> touch data_collector/management/__init__.py
> touch data_collector/management/commands/__init__.py
```

What these commands do is create a module called `management` under the `data_collector` module folder, and then create another module called `commands` in the `management` module. We do this by first creating the folders for the modules and then creating empty `__init__.py` files so that Python recognizes these folders as modules.

Next, let's try creating a simple management command that just prints out a list of the data points that we have in our database so far. Create a new `data_collector/management/commands/sample_data.py` file and give it the following content:

```python
from django.core.management import BaseCommand

from data_collector.models import DataPoint


class Command(BaseCommand):
    def handle(self, *args, **options):
        print('All data points:')
        print(DataPoint.objects.all())
```

Save this file and go back to your command prompt. Then run the following command:

```
> python manage.py sample_data
```

You should see the following output:

```
All data points:
[]
```

That's it. That's all there is to creating Django management commands. As you can see, we were able to use methods on our DataPoint model in a script that was run on the command line, as opposed to being run as part of an HTTP response view. A few things to note about Django management commands are as follows:

- Your command has the same name as the name of the file that contains the command.

- In order to be a valid management command, the source file should always define a Command class, which will be a base class of BaseCommand.

- Django will call the handle method of your Command class. This method is the starting point of whatever functionality you want to provide from your script.

We'll take a look at the *args and **options parameters next when we modify the sample_data.py command to actually add sample data. If you want further information about Django management commands, you should look at the documentation at https://docs.djangoproject.com/en/stable/howto/custom-management-commands/.

Let's modify our command class to add fake data. Here's the modified Command class code:

```python
class Command(BaseCommand):
    def add_arguments(self, parser):
        parser.add_argument('node_name', type=str)
        parser.add_argument('data_type', type=str)
        parser.add_argument('data_value', type=float)

    def handle(self, *args, **options):
        node_name = options['node_name']
        data_type = options['data_type']
        data_value = options['data_value']

        new_data_point = DataPoint(node_name=node_name, data_
type=data_type, data_value=data_value)
        new_data_point.save()

        print('All data points:')
        print(DataPoint.objects.all())
```

There are a couple of new things here. Let's look at the add_arguments method first. Most management commands need arguments to do something useful. As we're adding sample data to the database, our command will need the values to add. These are provided to the command in the form of arguments on the command line. If you don't have much experience with working with command lines, arguments are all the things that you type after the command name. For example, let's take a look at the command we use to create new Django applications in a project:

```
> python manage.py startapp APP_NAME
```

Here, we use the startapp Django management command, which is a built-in command, and the app name is an argument to the app.

We want our custom command to accept three arguments: the node name, data type, and value of the data point. In the add_arguments method, we tell Django to require and parse three arguments for this command.

The options parameter to the handle method is a dictionary that holds all the arguments that were defined and passed to the command by the user. In the handle method, we simply assign the values for each option to a variable. In case the user misses or adds extra arguments while calling the command, Django will print an error message as well as inform them of what the required parameters are. For example, if I call the command now without any parameter, here's what happens:

```
> python manage.py sample_data
usage: manage.py sample_data [-h] [--version] [-v {0,1,2,3}]
                             [--settings SETTINGS] [--pythonpath
PYTHONPATH]
                             [--traceback] [--no-color]
                             node_name data_type data_value
manage.py sample_data: error: the following arguments are required:
node_name, data_type, data_value
```

This is useful information if the user forgets how to use a management command.

Now that we have the argument values in variables, we create a new data point and save it. Finally, we print out all the data points that we have in the database. Let's try running our command now and see what output we get:

```
> python manage.py sample_data web01 load 5
All data points:
[<DataPoint: DataPoint object>]
```

While the command successfully created a new data point, the output isn't very helpful. We have no idea what information this data point holds. Let's fix this.

A better model representation

Whenever Django prints out a model instance, it first tries to see if there is a __str__ method defined for the model class. If it finds this method, it uses the output from it; otherwise, it falls back to a default implementation that just prints the class name, as we can see here. To make Django print out a more useful representation for our data point model, add this __str__ method to our DataPoint model class:

```
def __str__(self):
    return 'DataPoint for {}. {} = {}'.format(self.node_name, self.
data_type, self.data_value)
```

Let's run our sample_data command again now and see how its output has changed:

```
> python manage.py sample_data web01 load 1.0
All data points:
[<DataPoint: DataPoint for web01. load = 5.0>, <DataPoint: DataPoint
for web01. load = 1.0]
```

That's better. Now we see that the data point we added has been saved to the database correctly. Go ahead and create a couple of more data points. Use as many different node names as you want, but try to keep the data type limited to one of **load** or **disk_usage** as we'll be creating code specific to these data types later. Here's the sample data that I added to my database for reference:

Node name	Data type	Data value
web01	load	5.0
web01	load	1.0
web01	load	1.5
web01	disk_usage	0.5
web02	load	7.0
web02	load	9.0
web02	disk_usage	0.85
dbmaster	disk_usage	0.8
dbmaster	disk_usage	0.95

Now that we have a way to add sample data and added some to our database, let's create the status page that will show all this data to our users.

Status page

Our status page needs to show the user the status of their complete infrastructure in one view. To do so, a table feels like the appropriate design component. As the most important information to the user is going to be the latest status of their servers, our status page will need to show only one table row per node and list only the latest values for each different data type that we have in the database for that node.

For the sample data that I added to my database, we would ideally want a table similar to this on the status page:

Node Name	Metric	Value	Last Updated
web01	load	1.5	5 seconds ago
	disk_usage	0.5	now
web02	load	9.0	45 seconds ago
	disk_usage	0.85	5 minutes ago
dbmaster	disk_usage	0.95	10 seconds ago

As you can see, we only mention each node once, and group the different data types so that all information about a node is shown in one place and the user doesn't have to search through the table to find what they are looking for. As a bonus, we also show the last updated time in a nice way instead of just showing the time of the latest data point.

If you are thinking that showing our data points in a nice and consolidated manner like this will not be simple, I'm afraid you are right. We could get all the data points from the database in one query using `DataPoint.objects.all()` and then group them in our Python code, but that would be inefficient once the number of data points in our database grows. For server monitoring solutions, it isn't uncommon to have a couple of million data points. We can't go about getting and grouping all the million data points every time the user wants to see the status page. That would make loading the page unbearably slow.

Luckily for us, SQL—the language used to query data from databases—provides us with some very powerful constructs that we can use to get just the information we want, without having to go through all the rows of data that we could have in our data points table. Let's think about what we need.

For starters, we'd like to know the different node names in our database. For each node name, we also need to know the types of data that are available for it. In our example, while both **web01** and **web02** have the **load** and **disk_usage** data type available, the **dbmaster** node only has data for the **disk_usage** data type (or metric). For cases like this, the SQL language provides us with a DISTINCT query clause. Adding DISTINCT to our query instructs the database to return unique rows only. That is, all duplicate rows are only returned once. This way, we can get a list of all the different nodes and data types in our database without having to go over each record.

We need to experiment a bit to figure out how to translate the SQL query into something we can use with the Django ORM. We could write our view code and then keep changing it to figure out the right way to get the data we want, but that is very cumbersome. Instead, Django provides us with a very convenient shell to do these kinds of experimentations.

If you remember, at the start of this chapter, I showed you why you couldn't just start a Python shell and import the model. Django complained about not having been set up properly before being used. Instead, Django has its own way of launching a Python shell, one that makes sure that all the dependencies of setting up Django are met before you start using the shell. To start this shell, type the following:

```
> python manage.py shell
```

Like before, this will put you in a Python shell, which you can tell by the changed prompt. Now, let's try importing our DataPoint model:

```
>>> from data_collector.models import DataPoint
```

This time you shouldn't get any errors. Now type the following:

```
>>> DataPoint.objects.all()
[<DataPoint: DataPoint for web01. load = 5.0>, <DataPoint: DataPoint
for web01. load = 1.0>, <DataPoint: DataPoint for web01. load = 1.5>,
<DataPoint: DataPoint for web02. load = 7.0>, <DataPoint: DataPoint for
web02. load = 9.0>, <DataPoint: DataPoint for dbmaster. disk_usage =
0.8>, <DataPoint: DataPoint for dbmaster. disk_usage = 0.95>, <DataPoint:
DataPoint for web01. disk_usage = 0.5>, <DataPoint: DataPoint for web02.
disk_usage = 0.85>]
```

As you can see, you can query the model and see the output of the query immediately. The Django shell is one of the most useful components in Django, and you will often find yourself experimenting in the shell to figure out the correct way to do something before you write the final code in your views.

So, back to our problem of getting distinct node names and data types from our database. If you search the Django documentation for the **distinct** keyword, you should see this link in the results:

https://docs.djangoproject.com/en/stable/ref/models/
querysets/#distinct.

If you read what the documentation says, you should figure out that this is exactly what we need in order to use the DISTINCT clause. But how do we use it? Let's try it out in the shell:

```
>>> DataPoint.objects.all().distinct()
```

```
[<DataPoint: DataPoint for web01. load = 5.0>, <DataPoint: DataPoint
for web01. load = 1.0>, <DataPoint: DataPoint for web01. load = 1.5>,
<DataPoint: DataPoint for web02. load = 7.0>, <DataPoint: DataPoint for
web02. load = 9.0>, <DataPoint: DataPoint for dbmaster. disk_usage =
0.8>, <DataPoint: DataPoint for dbmaster. disk_usage = 0.95>, <DataPoint:
DataPoint for web01. disk_usage = 0.5>, <DataPoint: DataPoint for web02.
disk_usage = 0.85>]
```

Hmm? That didn't change anything. Why not? Let's think about what is happening here. We asked Django to query the database for all the data points and then return only one row for each duplicated data. If you are familiar with SQL, the distinct clause works by comparing each field in the rows of data you selected. However, as by default Django selects all the rows from a database table when querying a model, the data that the SQL query sees also includes the primary key, which is by definition unique for each row. This is why we see all of our data, even though we have used the distinct clause.

In order to make use of the distinct clause, we need to limit the fields in the data that we are asking the database to return to us. For our particular use case, we only need to know the unique pairs of node name and data type. The Django ORM provides another method, values, that we can use to limit the fields that Django selects. Let's try it out first without the distinct clause to see what data it returns:

```
>>> DataPoint.objects.all().values('node_name', 'data_type')
```

```
[{'data_type': u'load', 'node_name': u'web01'}, {'data_type': u'load',
'node_name': u'web01'}, {'data_type': u'load', 'node_name': u'web01'},
{'data_type': u'load', 'node_name': u'web02'}, {'data_type': u'load',
'node_name': u'web02'}, {'data_type': u'disk_usage', 'node_name':
u'dbmaster'}, {'data_type': u'disk_usage', 'node_name': u'dbmaster'},
{'data_type': u'disk_usage', 'node_name': u'web01'}, {'data_type':
u'disk_usage', 'node_name': u'web02'}]
```

That seems to do the trick. Now our data only includes the two fields that we wanted to run the distinct query on. Let's add the distinct clause as well and see what we get:

```
>>> DataPoint.objects.all().values('node_name', 'data_type').distinct()
[{'data_type': u'load', 'node_name': u'web01'}, {'data_type': u'load',
'node_name': u'web02'}, {'data_type': u'disk_usage', 'node_name':
u'dbmaster'}, {'data_type': u'disk_usage', 'node_name': u'web01'},
{'data_type': u'disk_usage', 'node_name': u'web02'}]
```

Voila! That seems to have done the trick. Now our Django ORM query only returns unique pairs of node names and data types, which is exactly what we needed.

One important thing to note is that after we added the `values` method to the ORM query, the returned data was no longer our `DataPoint` model class. Instead, it was dictionaries with just the field values that we asked for. Thus, any functions that you have defined on the model are not accessible on these dictionaries. If you think about it, this is obvious because without the complete fields, Django has no way to populate the model objects. It also won't matter if you listed all of your model fields in the `values` method arguments. It will still only return dictionaries, not the model objects.

Now that we have figured out how to get the data in the format we want, without having to loop over each row of data in our database, let's create the template, view, and URL configuration for our status page. Starting with the view code, change `data_collector/views.py` to have these contents:

```python
from django.views.generic import TemplateView

from data_collector.models import DataPoint


class StatusView(TemplateView):
    template_name = 'status.html'

    def get_context_data(self, **kwargs):
        ctx = super(StatusView, self).get_context_data(**kwargs)

        nodes_and_data_types = DataPoint.objects.all().values('node_
name', 'data_type').distinct()

        status_data_dict = dict()
        for node_and_data_type_pair in nodes_and_data_types:
            node_name = node_and_data_type_pair['node_name']
            data_type = node_and_data_type_pair['data_type']

            data_point_map = status_data_dict.setdefault(node_name,
dict())
```

```
        data_point_map[data_type] = DataPoint.objects.filter(
            node_name=node_name, data_type=data_type
        ).latest('datetime')

    ctx['status_data_dict'] = status_data_dict

    return ctx
```

It's a little complicated, so let's break it up into parts. First, we get a list of node name and data type pairs, using the query we came up with before. The result of the query, which we store in `nodes_and_data_types`, is similar to the following:

```
[{'data_type': u'load', 'node_name': u'web01'}, {'data_type': u'load',
'node_name': u'web02'}, {'data_type': u'disk_usage', 'node_name':
u'dbmaster'}, {
'data_type': u'disk_usage', 'node_name': u'web01'}, {'data_type':
u'disk_usage', 'node_name': u'web02'}]
```

As we've seen before, this is a list of all unique node name and data type pairs in our database. So, as our **dbmaster** node doesn't have any data for the **load** data type, you won't find that pair in this list. I'll explain in a while why running the distinct query helps us reduce the amount of load we need to put on our database.

Next, we loop over each of these pairs; that's the for loop you can see in the code. For each node name and data type pair, we run a query to get us the latest data point. First, we filter down to only the data points that we are interested in—those that match the node name and data type we specified. Then, we call the `latest` method and get the most recently updated data point.

The `latest` method takes the name of a field, orders the query using this field, and then returns the last row of data as per that ordering. It should be noted that `latest` can work with any field type that can be ordered, including numbers, not just date time fields.

I would like to point out the use of `setdefault` here. Calling `setdefault` on a dictionary makes sure that if the key provided doesn't exist in the dictionary already, the value passed as the second parameter is set for that key. This is a pretty useful pattern that I and a lot of Python programmers use when we are creating a dictionary in which all the keys need to have values of the same type—a dictionary in this case.

This allows us to ignore the scenario in which the key does not previously exist in the dictionary. Without using `setdefault`, we would first have to check whether the key exists. If it did, we would modify that. If it didn't, we would create a new dictionary, modify that, and then assign it to `status_data_dict`.

The `setdefault` method returns the value of the given key as well, whether it had to set it to the default value or not. We save that in the `data_point_map` variable in our code.

Finally, we add the `status_data_dict` dictionary to the context and return it. We'll see in our template how we go over this data and display it to the user. I said earlier that I would explain how the distinct query helped us reduce the load on the database. Let's look at an example scenario. Assume that we have the same three nodes in our infrastructure that we saw in our sample data: **web01**, **web02**, and **dbmaster**. Let's say that we have had monitoring running for one whole day, collecting stats for both load and disk usage on all three nodes every minute. Doing the math, we should have the following:

Number of nodes x number of data types x number of hours x 60:

```
3 x 2 x 24 x 60 = 8640
```

Thus, our data base has 8,640 data point objects. Now, with the code that we have in our view, we will only need to retrieve six data point objects from the database to show the user an updated status page plus the one distinct query. If we had to get all the data points, we would have to transfer the data for all those 8,640 data points from the database, and then use only six of them.

For the template, create a folder called `templates` in the `data_collector` directory. Then, create a `status.html` file in the template folder and give it the following content:

```
{% extends "base.html" %}

{% load humanize %}

{% block content %}
<h1>Status</h1>

<table>
    <tbody>
        <tr>
            <th>Node Name</th>
            <th>Metric</th>
            <th>Value</th>
            <th>Last Updated</th>
        </tr>

        {% for node_name, data_type_to_data_point_map in status_data_
dict.items %}
```

```
            {% for data_type, data_point in data_type_to_data_point_
map.items %}
            <tr>
                <td>{% if forloop.first %}{{ node_name }}{% endif %}</
td>
                <td>{{ data_type }}</td>
                <td>{{ data_point.data_value }}</td>
                <td>{{ data_point.datetime|naturaltime }}</td>
            </tr>
            {% endfor %}
        {% endfor %}
    </tbody>
</table>
{% endblock %}
```

There shouldn't be many surprises here. Ignoring the `load humanize` line, our template simply creates a table using the data dictionary that we generated in our view earlier. The two nested `for` loops might look a bit complicated, but looking at the data that we are looping over should make things clear:

```
{u'dbmaster': {u'disk_usage': <DataPoint: DataPoint for dbmaster.
disk_usage = 0.95>},
 u'web01': {u'disk_usage': <DataPoint: DataPoint for web01. disk_usage
= 0.5>,
            u'load': <DataPoint: DataPoint for web01. load = 1.5>},
 u'web02': {u'disk_usage': <DataPoint: DataPoint for web02. disk_usage
= 0.85>,
            u'load': <DataPoint: DataPoint for web02. load = 9.0>}}
```

The first for loop gets the node name and dictionary mapping data type to the latest data point. The inner for loop then iterates over the data type and the latest data point for the type and generates the table rows. We use the `forloop.first` flag to print the node name only if the inner loop is running for the first time. Django provides a few other useful flags related to for loops in templates. Take a look at the documentation at `https://docs.djangoproject.com/en/stable/ref/templates/builtins/#for`.

When we print the `datetime` field for a data point, we use the `naturaltime` filter. This filter is part of the humanize template tags provided as part of Django, which is why we needed to use the `load humanize` line at the start of the template. The `naturaltime` template filter outputs a date time value in a format that is easy for humans to understand, for example, two seconds ago, one hour ago, 20 minutes ago, and so on. You need to add `django.contrib.humanize` to the list of INSTALLED_APPS in `djagios/settings.py` before you can load the `humanize` template tags.

The final step in completing our status page is to add it to the URL configuration. As the status page is what the user wants to see most often from a monitoring system, let's make it the home page. Make the URL configuration file at `djagios/urls.py` contain the following content:

```
from django.conf.urls import url

from data_collector.views import StatusView


urlpatterns = [
    url(r'^$', StatusView.as_view(), name='status'),
]
```

That's it. Run the development server:

```
> python manage.py runserver
```

Access the status page at `http://127.0.0.1:8000`. If you have followed the steps so far, you should see a status page similar to the following one. Of course, your page will show data from your database:

Status

Node Name	Metric	Value	Last Updated
dbmaster	disk_usage	0.95	14 hours ago
web02	load	9.0	14 hours ago
	disk_usage	0.85	13 hours ago
web01	load	1.5	14 hours ago
	disk_usage	0.5	13 hours ago

Alerts

Now that we have a basic status page up and running, let's talk about allowing the user to configure some alert conditions. For now, we will inform the user of any alert condition by showing that node's information in red color on the status page.

First, we need to figure out what kind of alerts we want our users to set. From there, we can figure out the technical details. So, let's think about it. Given that the data types we are recording all have numeric values, it makes sense that the user should be able to set thresholds. They can, for instance, set an alert if the system load of any node goes above 1.0 or if the disk usage of a node goes above 80%.

Furthermore, maybe our users don't want to have the same alert conditions for each node. A database node is expected to handle a lot of system load, so maybe our users want to have a separate alert condition for the database node. Finally, if they are doing maintenance on some of the nodes, they may want to stop some alerts from triggering.

From all this, it seems that our alerts need to have fields to hold the following:

- Data type on which to trigger
- Maximum value to trigger on
- Minimum value to trigger on
- Node name to trigger on
- If the alert is currently active

Of these, the data type and active status are required fields that should never be null. The node name can be an empty string in which the alert conditions will be checked for each node. If the node name is not an empty string, it will be checked for nodes whose names match the provided string exactly.

As for the maximum and minimum values, one of those is required. This is so that the user may set alerts for just the maximum value without having to care about the minimum value for the data points. This will require manual validation in the model.

The model

Let's look at the model. To keep things simple, we'll use the `data_collector` app instead of creating a new one for alerts. Here is the code for our `Alert` model. Put this in `data_collector/models.py` after the `DataPoint` model code:

```
class Alert(models.Model):
    data_type = models.CharField(max_length=100)
    min_value = models.FloatField(null=True, blank=True)
```

```
    max_value = models.FloatField(null=True, blank=True)
    node_name = models.CharField(max_length=250, blank=True)

    is_active = models.BooleanField(default=True)

    def save(self, *args, **kwargs):
        if self.min_value is None and self.max_value is None:
            raise models.exceptions.ValidationError('Both min and max
value can not be empty for an alert')

        super(Alert, self).save(*args, **kwargs)
```

Due to our special requirements for the min and max fields, we had to override the
save method. As you can probably tell, our custom save method raises an error if
both the min and max values are not set. As there is no way to express this condition
with normal Django field configuration, we have to override the save method and
add our custom logic here. This is a pretty common thing to do in Django if you have
some custom validation requirements that depend on more than one field.

One more thing to note is the blank=True parameter to the min and max
FloatField. This is required so that any model forms constructed from this model,
which we will use for the create and update views later, allow blank values for
these fields.

Make and run migrations to add this to your database.

```
> python manage.py makemigrations data_collector
> python manage.py migrate data_collector
```

Management views

The users will need some views that they can use to manage alerts. They will need
pages to view all the alerts defined in the system, a page to create new alerts and edit
existing ones, and some way to delete alerts they no longer require. All of these are
achievable using the generic view provided by Django and some templates. Let's get
to it!

First, let's look at the list view first. Add this to data_collector/views.py:

```
class AlertListView(ListView):
    template_name = 'alerts_list.html'
    model = Alert
```

Remember to import `ListView` from `django.views.generic` and `Alert` from `data_collector.models`. Next, create the `alerts_list.html` template file in `data_collector/templates` and give it the following content:

```
{% extends "base.html" %}

{% block content %}
<h1>Defined Alerts</h1>

{% if object_list %}
<table>
    <tr>
        <th>Data Type</th>
        <th>Min Value</th>
        <th>Max Value</th>
        <th>Node Name</th>
        <th>Is Active</th>
    </tr>

    {% for alert in object_list %}
    <tr>
        <td>{{ alert.data_type }}</td>
        <td>{{ alert.min_value }}</td>
        <td>{{ alert.max_value }}</td>
        <td>{{ alert.node_name }}</td>
        <td>{{ alert.is_active }}</td>
    </tr>
    {% endfor %}
</table>
{% else %}
<i>No alerts defined</i>
{% endif %}
{% endblock %}
```

Finally, edit `djagios/urls.py`. Import the new view, and then add this to the URL patterns:

```
url(r'^alerts/$', AlertListView.as_view(), name='alerts-list'),
```

To test it out, open `http://127.0.0.1:8000/alerts/`. You should see the **No Alerts Defined** message. The list view is pretty basic. The `ListVew` generic view renders a template with all the objects for the specified model, providing the list of objects in the `object_list` template context variable. Next, let's look at the view to create new alerts.

In the `data_collector/view.py` file, first import the following:

```
from django.core.urlresolvers import reverse
from django.views.generic import CreateView
```

Then add this view class:

```
class NewAlertView(CreateView):
    template_name = 'create_or_update_alert.html'
    model = Alert
    fields = [
        'data_type', 'min_value', 'max_value', 'node_name', 'is_
active'
    ]

    def get_success_url(self):
        return reverse('alerts-list')
```

Nothing new in the view code. The template code is quite simple as well. Put this code in `data_collector/templates/create_or_update_alert.html`:

```
{% extends "base.html" %}

{% block content %}
{% if object %}
<h1>Update Alert</h1>
{% else %}
<h1>New Alert</h1>
{% endif %}

<form action="" method="post">{% csrf_token %}
    {{ form.as_p }}
    <input type="submit" value="{% if object %}Update{% else %}
Create{% endif %}" />
    <a href="{% url 'alerts-list' %}">Cancel</a>
</form>
{% endblock %}
```

As in previous chapters, we use the `object` context variable to decide if this template was used from `CreateView` or `UpdateView` and change some elements based on this. Otherwise, it's pretty straightforward. Let's see the code for `UpdateView` as well:

```
class EditAlertView(UpdateView):
    template_name = 'create_or_update_alert.html'
    model = Alert
    fields = [
```

```
                    'data_type', 'min_value', 'max_value', 'node_name', 'is_
active'
        ]

    def get_success_url(self):
        return reverse('alerts-list')
```

It's an almost identical copy of the previous create view. Make sure that you have imported the UpdateView generic view. We still need to add both of these views to our URL configuration. In the djagios/urls.py file, import both NewAlertView and EditAlertView and add these patterns:

```
url(r'^alerts/new/$', NewAlertView.as_view(), name='alerts-new'),
url(r'^alerts/(?P<pk>\d+)/edit/$', EditAlertView.as_view(),
name='alerts-edit'),
```

Before we can test these views, we should add links to allow users to get to these views. Modify the alerts_list.html template to match this code:

```
{% extends "base.html" %}

{% block content %}
<h1>Defined Alerts</h1>

{% if object_list %}
<table>
    <tr>
        <th>Data Type</th>
        <th>Min Value</th>
        <th>Max Value</th>
        <th>Node Name</th>
        <th>Is Active</th>
    </tr>

    {% for alert in object_list %}
    <tr>
        <td>{{ alert.data_type }}</td>
        <td>{{ alert.min_value }}</td>
        <td>{{ alert.max_value }}</td>
        <td>{{ alert.node_name }}</td>
        <td>{{ alert.is_active }}</td>
        <td><a href="{% url 'alerts-edit' pk=alert.pk %}">Edit</a></
td>
    </tr>
    {% endfor %}
</table>
```

```
{% else %}
<i>No alerts defined</i>
{% endif %}
<p><a href="{% url 'alerts-new' %}">Add New Alert</a></p>
{% endblock %}
```

Two new lines, which are highlighted, have been added. Now, let's see what our alerts list page looks like. As before, open `http://127.0.0.1:8000/alerts/` in your browser. You should see a page as follows:

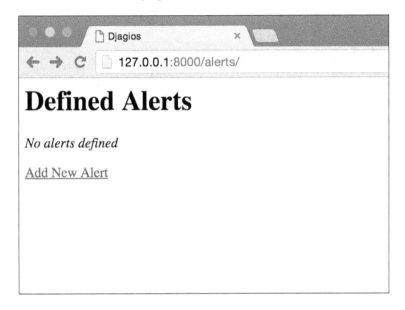

Click on the **Add New Alert** link and you should see the form to create an alert. Fill it in with some sample data and click on the **Create** button. If your form didn't have any errors, you should be back to the alerts list view and your screen should now list the new alert, as shown in the following screenshot:

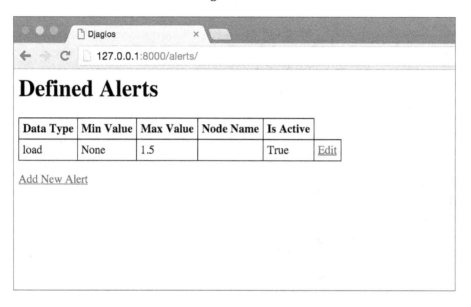

All that's left now is to allow users the option to delete their alerts. For this, create a view that subclasses from the generic `DeleteView`, remembering to import `DeleteView` from `django.views.generic` first. Here's the code you should put in `data_collector/view.py`:

```
class DeleteAlertView(DeleteView):
    template_name = 'delete_alert.html'
    model = Alert

    def get_success_url(self):
        return reverse('alerts-list')
```

Create a new `data_collector/templates/delete_alert.html` template:

```
{% extends "base.html" %}

{% block content %}
<h1>Delete alert?</h1>
<p>Are you sure you want to delete this alert?</p>
<form action="" method="post">{% csrf_token %}
    {{ form.as_p }}
```

```
      <input type="submit" value="Delete" />
      <a href="{% url 'alerts-list' %}">Cancel</a>
</form>
{% endblock %}
```

Next, import `DeleteAlertView` in `djagios/urls.py` and add this new pattern:

```
url(r'^alerts/(?P<pk>\d+)/delete/$', DeleteAlertView.as_view(),
name='alerts-delete'),
```

Finally, let's add a link to the delete view from the alerts list page. Edit the `alerts_list.html` template and add this line right after the **Edit** link:

```
<td><a href="{% url 'alerts-delete' pk=alert.pk %}">Delete</a></td>
```

Now when you open the alerts list view, you should see a **Delete** link. Your screen should look similar to the following screenshot:

If you click on the **Delete** link, you should see a confirmation page. If you confirm the deletion, you will see that your alert will be gone from the list page. These are all the views that we will need to manage alerts. Let's move on to detecting alert conditions and showing them in the status page.

Showing triggered alerts on the status page

As I said before, we want our users to see any nodes that have an alert triggered highlighted on the status page. Say that they defined an alert for when the disk usage on any node goes beyond 0.85 and the latest data point that we have for **dbmaster** disk usage has the value 0.9. When the user visits the status page, we would like the row showing the disk usage of the **dbmaster** node to be highlighted in red so that the user is immediately aware of the alert and is able to take actions to correct this.

Change StatusView in data_collector/view.py to match the following code. The changed bits are highlighted:

```
class StatusView(TemplateView):
    template_name = 'status.html'

    def get_context_data(self, **kwargs):
        ctx = super(StatusView, self).get_context_data(**kwargs)

        alerts = Alert.objects.filter(is_active=True)

        nodes_and_data_types = DataPoint.objects.all().values('node_
name', 'data_type').distinct()

        status_data_dict = dict()
        for node_and_data_type_pair in nodes_and_data_types:
            node_name = node_and_data_type_pair['node_name']
            data_type = node_and_data_type_pair['data_type']

            latest_data_point = DataPoint.objects.filter(node_
name=node_name, data_type=data_type).latest('datetime')
            latest_data_point.has_alert = self.does_have_alert(latest_
data_point, alerts)

            data_point_map = status_data_dict.setdefault(node_name,
dict())
            data_point_map[data_type] = latest_data_point

        ctx['status_data_dict'] = status_data_dict

        return ctx

    def does_have_alert(self, data_point, alerts):
```

```
    for alert in alerts:
        if alert.node_name and data_point.node_name != alert.node_
name:
            continue

        if alert.data_type != data_point.data_type:
            continue

        if alert.min_value is not None and data_point.data_value <
alert.min_value:
            return True
        if alert.max_value is not None and data_point.data_value >
alert.max_value:
            return True

    return False
```

What we have done here is to check, for each data point that we retrieve, whether it triggers any alert. We do this by comparing the min and max values in every alert with the data point value, but only if the data point data type and node name match those in the alert. If the data point value is outside of the alert range, we mark the data point as having triggered an alert.

This is another technique often used by me in a number of projects I've done. As models are just Python objects, you can attach extra information to them on the fly. No need to define `has_alert` on the `DataPoint` class. Just add it to the objects when needed. Be careful though. It's not a good programming practice to do something like this, because someone trying to understand the `DataPoint` class will have no idea that the `has_alert` attribute event exists unless they look at the code for the view class. As we only use this attribute in the view and template, it's fine for us. However, if we passed the `DataPoint` objects around and more code started using this attribute, it would be much better to define it on the class itself so that anyone looking at the class code would know it existed.

We need to modify the `status.html` template as well to make use of the `has_alert` attribute that we have added to the data points. Change it to match the following code. As before, the modified portions have been highlighted:

```
{% extends "base.html" %}

{% load humanize %}

{% block content %}
<h1>Status</h1>

<table>
    <tbody>
        <tr>
            <th>Node Name</th>
            <th>Metric</th>
            <th>Value</th>
            <th>Last Updated</th>
        </tr>

        {% for node_name, data_type_to_data_point_map in status_data_
dict.items %}
            {% for data_type, data_point in data_type_to_data_point_
map.items %}
            <tr {% if data_point.has_alert %}class="has-alert"{% endif
%}>
                <td>{% if forloop.first %}{{ node_name }}{% endif %}</
td>
                <td>{{ data_type }}</td>
                <td>{{ data_point.data_value }}</td>
                <td>{{ data_point.datetime|naturaltime }}</td>
            </tr>
            {% endfor %}
        {% endfor %}
    </tbody>
</table>

<style type="text/css" media="all">
    tr.has-alert td:not(:first-child) {
        color: red;
    }
</style>
{% endblock %}
```

That's it. In order to test it out, you need to create some `Alert` objects that will be triggered by `DataPoints` in your database. For the sample data that I used, I created one `Alert` object with the **disk_usage** data type and a max value of 0.5. After creating the alert, my status screen highlighted the nodes that triggered the alert. You screen will show something similar:

To test whether our highlighting code works correctly, I added another data point for the **dbmaster** disk usage metric, using the following command:

```
> python manage.py sample_data dbmaster disk_usage 0.2
```

After refreshing the status page, the alert condition for the **dbmaster** node disappeared. You should do a similar test to see for yourself.

That's it! It's been hard work, but our monitoring tool is now starting to shape up. We have a status page that shows the latest node statuses, highlighting any that have alerts. The highlights disappear once the alert condition is resolved. We have a page to manage our alerts as well. All in all, we can say that the user-facing parts of the application are almost finished. One thing that would be pretty helpful is a navigation bar. Add this just after the start of the body tag in `templates/base.html`:

```html
<ul>
    <li><a href="{% url 'status' %}">Home</a></li>
    <li><a href="{% url 'alerts-list' %}">Alerts</a></li>
</ul>
```

Refresh the status page and you should see a simple navigation menu at the top of the page.

Accepting data from remote systems

Now that users can see the status of their infrastructure and manage alerts, it's time to move on to the next step: getting data from real sources instead of using Django management commands to input sample data.

To do so, we will create an API **endpoint** that accepts data from remote systems. An API endpoint is just a fancy name for a Django view that doesn't have a template to render. The response from an API endpoint is typically either just a 200 OK status or a JSON response. API endpoints are not meant to be used by human users. Instead, they are meant to be used by different software systems to connect together and share information.

The API endpoint that we need to create will be a simple view that accepts a POST request with all the information needed to create a new `DataPoint` object. To make sure that malicious users can't spam our database with random data, we will also add a simple authentication mechanism to our API endpoint so that it will accept data only from authorized sources.

To create an API endpoint, we'll use the `django.view.generic.View` class, implementing only the POST handler. To parse the request data, we'll be creating a model form on the fly. Edit `data_collector/views.py` and add the following code:

```
from django.forms.models import modelform_factory
from django.http.response import HttpResponse
from django.http.response import HttpResponseBadRequest
from django.http.response import HttpResponseForbidden
from django.views.generic import View


class RecordDataApiView(View):
    def post(self, request, *args, **kwargs):
        # Check if the secret key matches
        if request.META.get('HTTP_AUTH_SECRET') != 'supersecretkey':
            return HttpResponseForbidden('Auth key incorrect')

        form_class = modelform_factory(DataPoint, fields=['node_name',
'data_type', 'data_value'])
        form = form_class(request.POST)
        if form.is_valid():
```

```
        form.save()
        return HttpResponse()
    else:
        return HttpResponseBadRequest()
```

There are a couple of new things here that we need to look at. Firstly, we have used the META attribute on the request object to access a request. If you have knowledge of how the HTTP protocol works, you should be familiar with headers. If not, a good explanation is available at `https://www.jmarshall.com/easy/http/`. Explaining headers in detail is beyond the scope of this book, but simply stated, headers are extra pieces of information added to an HTTP request by the client. We'll see how to add them in the next section when we test our API view.

Django automatically normalizes all header names and adds them to the META dictionary. Here, we are using a custom header **Auth-Secret** to make sure that only clients that have our secret key can use this view.

> More information about what goes into the META dictionary and how it is consturcted is available in the Django docs at `https://docs.djangoproject.com/en/stable/ref/request-response/#django.http.HttpRequest.META`.

The next thing that we need to look at is the modelform_factory function. It's a neat little function provided by Django that returns a ModelForm subclass for the given model. You can customize the model form to a certain degree using the arguments to this function. Here, we limit the number of fields that can be edited. Why use a model form in the first place?

What we wanted from the API endpoint was a method to create new DataPoint models. Model forms provide exactly the functionality that we need to do this plus they handle data validation for us. We could have created a separate model form class in a forms.py file and then used that in our view as we have done before, but there are two reasons we didn't.

Firstly, this was the only place in our code where we use a model form for the DataPoint method. If we needed to use it in other places as well, defining the model form in a single place would be the best programming practice. However, as we don't, we can get away with defining the model form dynamically where we need it.

Secondly, we didn't need any customizations to the model form class. If we wanted to, say, override the save method as we've done previously, we would have been forced to define the class instead of using the modelform_factory method.

After getting the model form class, we use it like any model form class to either create the new data point or return a response indicating that the data validation failed. To make our new endpoint available via a URL, import the following in `djagios/urls.py`:

```
from django.views.decorators.csrf import csrf_exempt
from data_collector.views import RecordDataApiView
```

Then, add this URL pattern:

```
url(r'^record/$', csrf_exempt(RecordDataApiView.as_view()),
    name='record-data'),
```

The `csrf_exempt` decorator is used because, by default, Django uses CSRF protection for POST requests. However, this is usually used on web forms, not API endpoints. So we have to disable it, otherwise Django won't allow our POST request to succeed. Now, let's look at how to test out our new view.

 You can get more information about CSRF protection provided by Django at `https://docs.djangoproject.com/en/stable/ref/csrf/`.

Testing API endpoints

You can't simply test this API endpoint in your browser because it's a POST request and there's no template that can render a form in your browser. However, a lot of great tools are available to make manual POST requests. The one that I suggest you use is Postman. It's a Google Chrome app, so you don't need to install any dependencies. As long as you have Google Chrome installed on your machine, you can get Postman from `https://www.getpostman.com/`. After you have installed it, start it up and you should see a screen similar to the following one. Don't worry if your Postman screen isn't exactly the same. It can be that the version you downloaded is a newer one. The main parts of Postman should be the same.

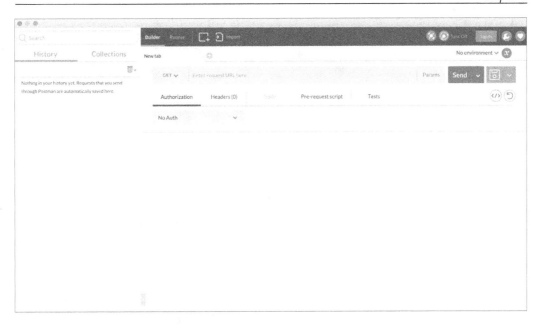

Using Postman is simple. I will walk you through the entire process step by step, including an image for each step to make it clear what I mean. At the end of this process, we should be able to use our API endpoint to generate a new data point.

As a side note, if you are using a Linux- or Unix-based OS, such as Ubuntu or Mac OS X, and are more comfortable using the command line, you can use the `curl` utility to make the POST request. It is usually faster for simpler requests. To make the same request using `curl` as the one I demonstrate here in Postman, type this on your command prompt:

```
> curl http://127.0.0.1:8000/record/ -H 'Auth-Secret: supersecretkey' -d
node_name=web01 -d data_type=disk_usage -d data_value=0.2
```

To make this request using Postman, perform the following steps:

1. Select the request type. We want to make a POST request, so select POST from the drop-down menu:

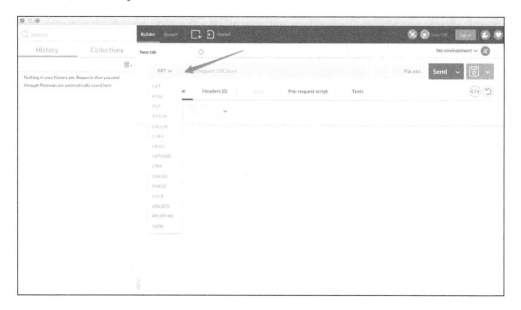

2. Enter the URL you want to make the request to. In our case, it is `http://127.0.0.1:8000/record/`:

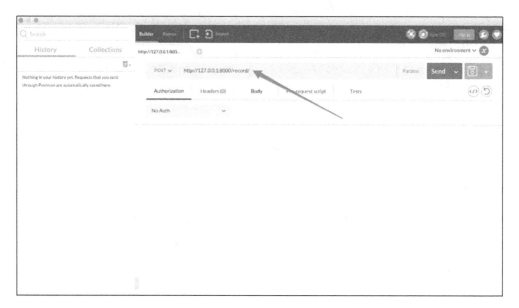

3. Add our custom authentication header. Open up the **Headers** tab and add the **Auth-Secret** header with a value of **supersecretkey**:

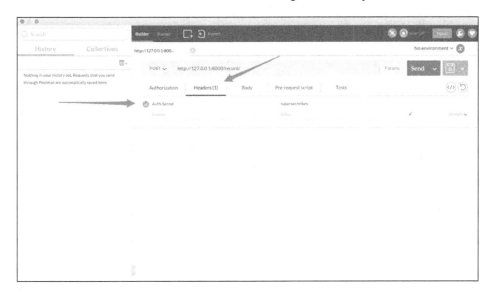

4. Finally, add our POST parameters to the **Body** section. The sample data that I used was as follows:

   ° node_name: web01

   ° data_type: disk_usage

   ° data_value: 0.72

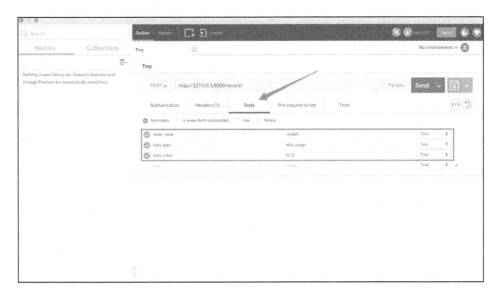

That's it. Our request is now set up. Click on the **Send** button next to the URL textbox and you should see an empty response below the body parameters. To confirm that the request worked properly, look at the status code of the response. It should be **200 OK**:

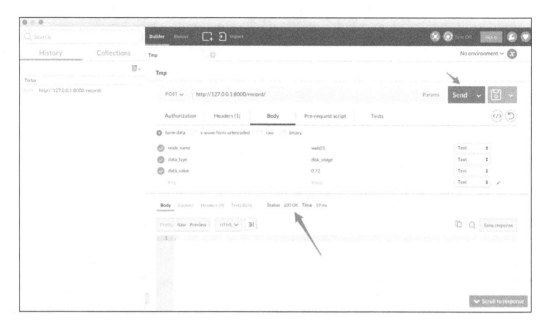

Open up the status page for our application at `http://127.0.0.1:8000/` and you should see the latest data point value displayed there. That's it, we're done!

> As explained at the start of this section, you can also use command-line tools such as `curl` to upload data to the API. Using such tools, you can come up with shell scripts that automatically update the web app with real data from your computer systems. This is how Nagios and a lot of data monitoring tools operate as well. The servers have API endpoints that listen for data, and then simple scripts gather and upload data to the servers from the client nodes.

Summary

This was a pretty demanding chapter, and you learned a lot of new information.

For starters, we looked at Django management commands. They are an important feature of Django. All Django commands that you run, such as `python manage.py startapp`, are management commands as well, so you should already know how powerful they can be. In bigger projects, you almost always have a few management commands to automate your tasks for you.

We also looked at how Django creates a string representation of our models using the `__str__` method on our model class. It's not just used when printing to the console either. Any time you try to use your model objects as strings, even in your templates, Django uses this representation, so it's important to have a good format that can immediately give you all the important information about an object.

This chapter also introduced advance query methods, specifically the `distinct` and `values` methods that allow you to issue more complicated SQL queries to get data in exactly the format you want from the database. However, this is just the beginning. In later chapters, we might need to use more complicated query methods. You might want to look at the Django documentation for `queryset` methods at `https://docs.djangoproject.com/en/stable/ref/models/querysets/` to learn about more methods of querying the databases that Django provides.

In addition to getting data from the database in a format that we wanted, we also looked at preparing a somewhat complicated data structure with the data to pass all the required information to templates, and then saw how to use that data structure in our templates.

Often, you have complicated data validation rules that you need to ensure are passing before you can save data to a database. We looked at how to achieve this in this chapter by overriding the `save` method of our model classes.

Finally, you learned how to create simple API endpoints and how to test them using `curl` or Postman. Overall, this was a big chapter that introduced a lot of new concepts that will be used in later chapters.

4

A Car Rental App

For this chapter, our hypothetical client is a car rental firm. They want us to create a website that their customers can visit, look at the available inventory of cars, and finally book one of those cars. The client also wants an admin panel where they can manage the inventory and booking requests.

We will be creating this web app in (drum rolls) Django! You should be confident enough in Django by now that the frontend of the web app will not be a challenge for us. The focus of this chapter will be on customizing the Django built-in **admin** app to fit the requirements of our client. Most of the time when you need an administration panel for the web apps you create, you can do pretty much everything you need just by customizing the Django admin. Sometimes the requirements are complex enough that you need to create a custom administration panel, but that is seldom the case. So the knowledge we gain here will prove extremely useful to you in your web development career.

The main takeaways from this chapter will be as follows:

- Customizing Django admin model forms
- Adding custom filters to the admin objects list page
- Overriding and customizing Django admin templates

Code pack

As I have mentioned, by now you should have a firm grasp of creating the components for a basic web app, including the views, templates, models, and URL configurations, so we will not be discussing these parts of the web app in this chapter. The code pack for this chapter is thus much bigger that the previous ones. I have created all the models and some of the views, templates, and URLs. We will mostly be focusing on how to tame the Django admin app to suit our needs.

I could not think of a fancy name for this project, so I just called the project *carrental*. As always, create a new virtual environment, install Django in this environment, and run the migrate command to initialize the database. For this project, we need to install one more Python package, Pillow, which is an image manipulation library for Python. To install it, run the following command with the virtual environment activated:

```
> pip install Pillow
```

This might take a minute or so as some compilation may be required. Installing Pillow is a bit more complicated because it relies on third-party libraries. If the install command fails for you, take a look at the documentation on installing Pillow at `https://pillow.readthedocs.org/en/3.0.x/installation.html`. This page has step-by-step guides for each operating system, and following the guide there, you should be able to install Pillow easily. Just remember that you need the library to run and work on the car rental application.

Once Pillow has been installed, run the development server using the `runserver` command and open up the web app at `http://127.0.0.1:8000`. You should see the following page:

Fixtures

Our database is empty, but right now we don't have any views to add objects to our database. We could do what we did in the last chapter and create a management command, but there's an easier way. I have added three `Car` objects to the database and then created a dump of this data that you can load. A data dump like this is called a fixture. We'll discuss fixtures in a bit; for now, let's see how to use them to load data in our database.

On your command line, run this command in the project root with the virtual environment activated:

```
> python manage.py loaddata frontend/fixtures/initial.json
Installed 3 object(s) from 1 fixture(s)
```

Refresh the web page and now you should see a web page similar to this:

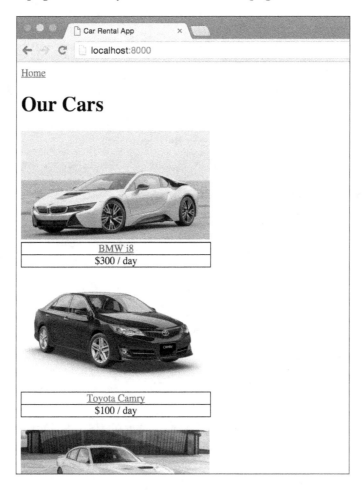

Now we have three cars in our database. You should play around the app for a while. It has a details page for each car and allows you to submit a booking request from the details page.

> If you try to use the booking form, note that the start and end dates need to be in the YYYY-MM-DD format. For example, 2016-12-22 is a valid date format accepted by the form.

To learn more about fixtures, take a look at the Django documentation at `https://docs.djangoproject.com/en/stable/howto/initial-data/`. Fixtures are a feature of Django that let you dump the data in your database in simple text files using a number of formats. The most commonly used format is JSON. Once you have a fixture file, you can then use it to populate your database with data, as we did here, using the `loaddata` command.

Before we move on to admin customization, I want to talk about a couple of new things that I have used in the models for this app. You should take a look at `frontend/models.py` to see how our models are configured, and then read the following information, which explains the new concepts.

Image and File fields

I'd like to take a minute to introduce the `ImageField` model field. This is the first time we are seeing it, and using it is a bit different than other model fields. Here is our `Car` model that uses this field:

```python
class Car(models.Model):
    name = models.CharField(max_length=100)
    image = models.ImageField(upload_to='car_images')
    description = models.TextField()
    daily_rent = models.IntegerField()

    is_available = models.BooleanField()

    def get_absolute_url(self):
        return reverse('car-details', kwargs={'pk': self.pk})
```

> All of the information in this section about `ImageField` also relates to `FileField`.

`ImageField` is special and different from all the other database model fields that we have looked at for a few reasons. Firstly, it needs the Pillow image manipulation library to work, which is why we had to install it at the start of the chapter. If we had tried to run our application without Pillow installed, Django would have complained and never started the development server.

Secondly, `ImageField` is one of the few Django database model fields that relies on having a few settings configured before it can be used. If you look at the `carrental/settings.py` file near the end, you should see that I have set the `MEDIA_ROOT` and `MEDIA_URL` variables.

Lastly, you can see that we passed a `upload_do` parameter to `ImageField` and set it to `car_images`. Both `FileField` and `ImageField` database model fields require this parameter. This parameter is the name of the folder, relative to the configured `MEDIA_ROOT`, where any files being uploaded to your application through the Image/File fields will be saved. This is a concept that took me some time to figure out, so I'll explain it a bit further.

You should see that I have `MEDIA_ROOT` set to the `media` folder in the project root. If you take a look in the `media` folder, you should see another folder called `car_images`. This is the same name that we passed in the `upload_to` parameter. This is what I meant when I said that the `upload_to` parameter is a folder name *relative* to the configured media root.

> One thing I had trouble understanding when I started using Django was the difference between `MEDIA_ROOT` and `STATIC_ROOT`. To put it simply, `MEDIA_ROOT` is where all the files uploaded by the site users live. These files are uploaded using the Image/File fields with forms.
>
> `STATIC_ROOT` is where you put the static files associated with your web applications. These include CSS files, JavaScript files, and any other static files that are served as is. These have nothing to do with the Django part of your web application; these are delivered to the user as is, usually via a web server such as nginx.

So now that you have everything configured, how do you upload files using `ImageField`? Well, Django supports a couple of different ways to do this. In our code, we will use `ModelForm`, which handles all the details for us. There are other ways as well. If you want further details, you should look at the Django documentation dealing with file uploads. It's quite comprehensive and lists all the different ways you can handle file uploads. You can refer to it at `https://docs.djangoproject.com/en/stable/topics/http/file-uploads/`.

get_absolute_url

One more thing that we are seeing for the first time in the `Car` model is `get_absolute_url`. There is nothing special about the implementation. It's just a class method that returns a URL, which it builds using the `reverse` function and the primary key of the object. This isn't anything new. We have been creating URLs like this for detail pages since the first chapter. What's interesting to note here is that Django assigns special meaning to the `get_absolute_url` method on a model class. There are a number of places where Django will automatically use the return value of the `get_absolute_url` method if the method exists on a model object. For instance, the `CreateView` generic method uses it. If you do not provide a `success_url` attribute and a custom `get_success_url` method on the view class, Django will try to get the URL to redirect from the `get_absolute_url` method on the newly created object if the method is defined in the model class.

Django also uses this method in the admin app, as we'll see later on. If you are interested, you can take a look at the documentation for it:

`https://docs.djangoproject.com/en/stable/ref/models/instances/#get-absolute-url/`.

The Django admin app

Now that we have looked at what new features were used in the code pack, let's move on to the main topic for this chapter—the Django **admin** app. The admin app is quite possibly one of the main reasons for the popularity of Django over other similar web frameworks. It is the embodiment of the *batteries included* nature of Django. With minimal configuration, the admin app provides a fully featured and extremely tailored CMS, enough to rival big names such as WordPress and Drupal.

In this chapter, you will learn how easy it is to configure and customize the admin to get most of the functionality that you will want in the admin panels of your web apps. Let's start by fixing the most immediate problem for our fictional client, a car rental business owner, which is the ability to add and edit car details.

When you start a new application, Django by default creates an `admin.py` file in the application folder. Change the `frontend/admin.py` file in our project to match this content:

```
from django.contrib import admin
from frontend.models import Car
admin.site.register(Car)
```

That's it. Really! Three lines in total and you get the ability to edit and add `Car` objects to your database. That's the power of Django, right there in those three lines. Let's test it out. In your browser, visit `http://127.0.0.1:8000/admin` and you should see a page similar to the following one:

 Don't worry if your admin looks slightly different. Django updates the theme for the admin every once in a while and, depending on which version of Django you are using, your admin may look slightly different. However, all the functionality will be there and will almost always have the same interface layout.

Oops, there is one thing that we left out. We didn't create a user to log in with. This is easily fixable. In the command line, run this command with the virtual environment activated:

```
> python manage.py createsuperuser
```

Just follow along with the prompts to create a new user. Once you have created the user, use it to log in to the admin. After logging in, you should see something similar to this:

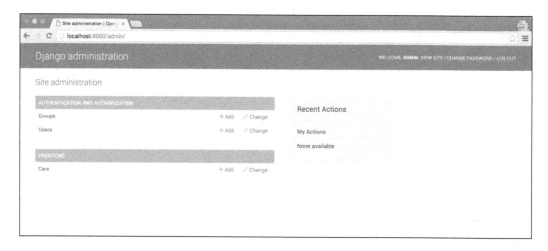

A few things to note in this screen. First, Django will by default add links to manage **Groups** and **Users**. Secondly, any models that we configure to show up in the admin are grouped by their application name. Thus, the link to manage **Cars** shows up under the label for the app that defines the model, **Frontend**.

If you pay close attention, you might note that the admin lists the plural name of our Car model. How does it know the plural name? Well, it simply adds an 's' in front of our model name. In a lot of cases, this doesn't work, for instance, if we had a model called Bus. For cases like this, Django allows us to configure the plural name for a model.

Let's try editing one of the car objects that we have in our database. Click on the **Cars** link and you should see a screen similar to the following one:

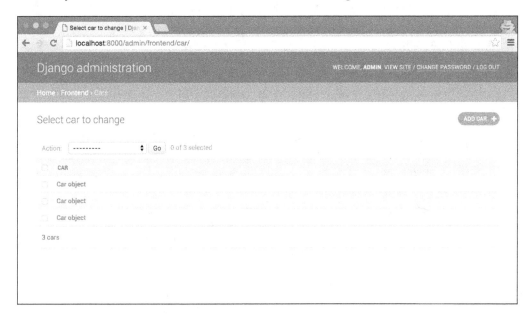

The list doesn't look very useful. We have no idea which car object is which. We'll fix this in a bit. For now, just click on the top car object in the list, and you should see a page where you can edit the details for that object:

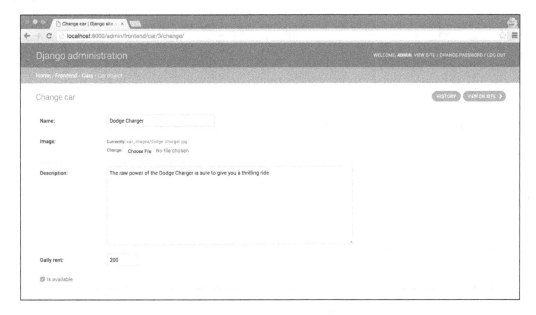

The Django admin docs refer to this list as changelist. I will just call it the list view in this chapter.

Let's change the name of the car. I changed **Dodge Charger** to **My New Car Name**. Scroll to the bottom of the page after changing the name and click on save. To make sure that our changes were actually saved, open the home page for our app at `http://127.0.0.1:8000/` and you'll see that the car you edited will have the new name displayed.

Let's try something more complicated—adding a new car! Click on the **ADD CAR** button on the right-hand side of the screen and fill in the details however you want. Just be sure to select the `is_available` checkbox; otherwise, the new car won't show up on the home page. I filled up the form as shown in this screenshot:

I also downloaded an image for the car from Google Images and selected it for the **Image** field. Click on the save button and visit the home page again. The new car you added should show up at the end of the list:

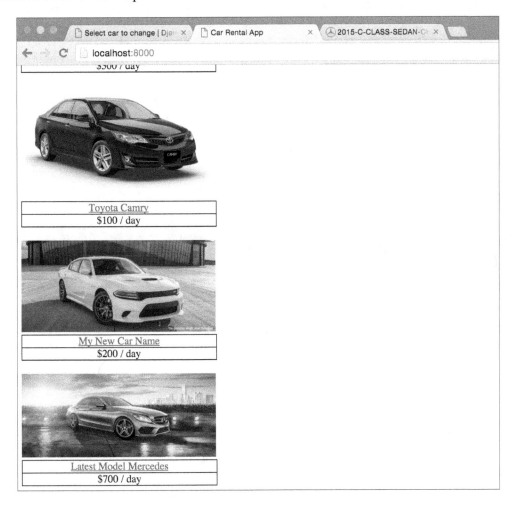

As I mentioned at the start of this section, the power of the Django admin is one of the main reasons for Django's popularity. By now you should see why. In three lines, we have a complete and working, albeit not very pretty, content management system that the client can use to edit and add cars to their site.

However, in its current form, the admin looks like a quick hack job. The client will probably not be very happy with this. They can't even see which car they are about to edit before the edit page opens up. Let's fix this first. We will come back to the code we just wrote for the admin in a bit.

Showing the car names

If you remember in the previous chapter, we looked at the __str__ method on a model class. I also said that Django uses this method wherever it needs to display a string representation of the model. Well, that's exactly what the Django admin does in the list view for the Car model: it displays the string representation for it. Let's make the list more user friendly by changing the string representation to something that the user can understand. In the frontend/models.py file, add this __str__ method to the Car model class:

```
def __str__(self):
    return self.name
```

Let's see what the list of Car objects looks now:

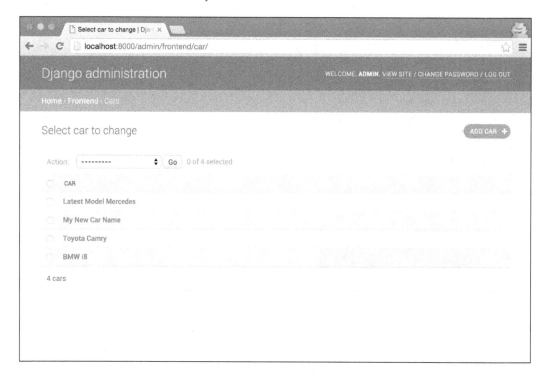

That's a much better user experience as the user can now see which car they are about to edit.

Booking management

Let's leave the car admin section as it is for now and move on to the admin for `Booking` model. Every time a visitor to the site submits the **Book Now** form accessible from the car details page, we create a new `Booking` model record. We need a way to allow the client to look at these booking enquiries, filter them based on some criteria, and accept or reject them. Let's look at how to do this. For a start, let's make sure that our The `Booking` model shows up as an item in our admin panel. To do so, add these two lines to your `frontend/admin.py` file:

```
from frontend.models import Booking
admin.site.register(Booking)
```

If you take a look at the admin panel now at the URL `http://127.0.0.1:8000/admin/`, you should see that the `Booking` model has been added as a link. Open up the link and you should see a list page similar to the one for the `Car` model that we saw before. If you had submitted any booking requests, they should show up in the list. It's not pretty, but at least it works. Let's make it better. For one, we need to give the administrators more information about each booking enquiry. It will be good if we can show the customer's name, booking start and end dates, and whether the booking has already been approved.

While we could use the `__str__` method again to create a string with all this information, so much information in one column isn't a pretty sight. Additionally, we would be missing out on the sorting capabilities that the Django admin provides us with for each model list page.

Let's look at how we can display multiple fields from our model in the list view. Along the way, you will also learn a bit more about how the admin works internally.

A peek behind the curtain

If you take a minute to think about what we have been able to achieve with just a couple of lines of code, you would probably be amazed at the power of the Django admin. How is this power achieved? Well, the answer to that is very complicated. Even I don't yet understand fully how the admin app works. It is a very complex piece of programming.

> Even though the admin app is quite complex, it is still Python code. If you're feeling adventurous or just generally bored one day, try to look at the source code for the admin app. It's in the `VIRTUAL_ENV/lib/python3.5/site-packages/django/contrib/admin` folder. Replace `VIRTUAL_ENV` with the folder that holds the virtual environments you create for your projects.

One of the main components of the admin system is the `ModelAdmin` class. Just as the `models.Model` class allows us to define complicated database models using a very simple class definition, the `ModelAdmin` class allows us to customize the admin interface for a model in great detail. Let's see how we can use it to add extra fields to our list of booking enquiries. Change the `frontend/admin.py` file to match the following contents:

```
from django.contrib import admin

from frontend.models import Car
from frontend.models import Booking


class BookingModelAdmin(admin.ModelAdmin):
    list_display = ['customer_name', 'booking_start_date', 'booking_
end_date', 'is_approved']


admin.site.register(Car)
admin.site.register(Booking, BookingModelAdmin)
```

Now if you open up the admin list page for the `Booking` model, you should see something similar to this with all the important fields displayed:

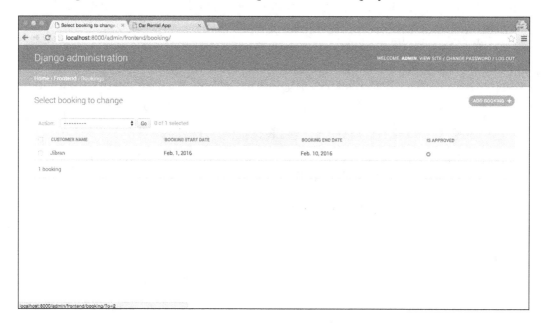

This presents the user with a very nice tabular view. The client now sees all of the relevant details and has the ability to sort the table according to their needs. Django is also helpful enough to show the date values in a nice format. Let's look at what we have done here.

We first created a `ModelAdmin` subclass called `BookingModelAdmin`. We then configured the fields that we would like to show in the list page using the `list_display` attribute. Finally, we need to associate our `ModelAdmin` class with the `Booking` model class so that the admin can customize itself according to our requirements. We do that using the following:

```
admin.site.register(Booking, BookingModelAdmin)
```

If you look at how we register the `Car` model, it looks similar to the `Booking` model:

```
admin.site.register(Car)
```

That's because it is the same thing. If you don't provide a custom `ModelAdmin` subclass, Django uses the default options, which is what we see with the `Car` model.

Improving the user experience

While we have improved upon the base admin interface quite a bit just by showing the relevant fields on the list page, we can do more. Let's look at some actions that an administrator might want to take for the booking enquiries that the site receives:

- Viewing only the booking enquiries that have been approved or the ones that have not yet been approved

- Searching for a booking by customer name

- Approving or not approving a booking enquiry quickly

- Selecting multiple booking enquiry objects and sending e-mails to the customers about their approval/disapproval

Filtering objects

For our first feature, we want to allow the user filtering on the displayed objects. There should be a filter on the page that allows them to see only bookings that have been approved or not approved. To do so, the Django admin provides you with a `list_filter` attribute on the `ModelAdmin` subclass. The `list_filter` attribute holds a list of fields that you can filter on. In our `BookingModelAdmin` class, add the following `list_filter` attribute:

```
list_filter = ['is_approved']
```

That's it. Once you have added this line to `BookingModelAdmin`, open up the bookings list page; on the right-hand side, you should see a new sidebar where you can select which bookings you want to view — only those that are approved or those that are not approved, or both. It should look similar to the following screenshot:

Searching for objects

Just as the Django admin has built-in support for filters, it also provides an easy-to-use way to add search. We want our client to be able to search bookings by the customer name field. To do so, add the `search_fields` attribute to the `BookingModelAdmin` class:

```
search_fields = ['customer_name']
```

That's it. Once you have added this attribute, you should see a search box at the top of the booking objects list. Type in a few sample queries and see how it works. If you have more than one field that you want to make searchable, you can add that to the list of `search_fields` as well.

If you have more than one field name in the list, Django will do an OR search. This simply means that for a given search, ALL records that have at least ONE matching field value will show.

Quick edit

The third feature on our list is to allow admins to quickly mark a booking as approved/not approved. The Django admin provides another built-in feature that we can configure to get what we need. In your `BookingModelAdmin` class, add the `list_editable` attribute:

```
list_editable = ['is_approved']
```

If you open the booking list page now, you will notice that instead of the icon that was shown in the is_approved column before, you now have a checkbox and a **Save** button added at the end of the list. You can select the checkboxes for bookings you want to approve and deselect it for the ones you want to disapprove, and click on **Save**. Django will then save your changes to multiple objects in one go.

By now, our Booking list page looks similar to the following screenshot:

Admin actions

The last thing on our list of features is the ability for the user to select multiple booking enquiry objects and send out an e-mail to customer_email for each Booking object containing the approval status of the booking. For now, we will just print out the e-mail on the console to test this feature out. We will look at sending e-mails from Django in a later chapter.

Until now, most of the editing that we did with the Django admin was on a per object basis. You select an object, edit it, then save it, and start over. Except for the last feature (quick edit), we have been editing objects one at a time. However, sometimes you want the ability to perform a common action on multiple objects, like we need with our e-mail feature. To implement features like these, the Django admin provides **Admin Actions**.

Admin actions are methods on the ModelAdmin class that are passed a list of objects that the user has selected. These methods can then take some action on each of these objects and return the user to the changelist page again.

Actually, I am simplifying this a bit. Admin actions don't need to be methods on `ModelAdmin`. They can be standalone functions as well. However, it's usually a good programming practice to declare them in `ModelAdmin` that uses them, so that's how we will do it here. You can find more details in the documentation for admin actions at `https://docs.djangoproject.com/en/stable/ref/contrib/admin/actions/`.

The Django admin by default provides one action: delete. If you open the **Action** drop-down at the top of the list of bookings, you should see this menu:

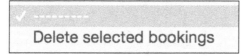

To define an admin action, you first need to create a method on the `ModelAdmin` class and then add the name of the method to the `actions` attribute on the class. The `actions` attribute is a list like all the other attributes that we have seen till now. Modify the `BookingModelAdmin` to match the following code:

```
class BookingModelAdmin(admin.ModelAdmin):
    list_display = ['customer_name', 'booking_start_date', 'booking_
end_date', 'is_approved']
    list_filter = ['is_approved']
    list_editable = ['is_approved']
    search_fields = ['customer_name']

    actions = ['email_customers']

    def email_customers(self, request, queryset):
        for booking in queryset:
            if booking.is_approved:
                email_body = """Dear {},
    We are pleased to inform you that your booking has been approved.
Thanks
""".format(booking.customer_name)
            else:
                email_body = """Dear {},
    Unfortunately we do not have the capacity right now to accept your
booking.
Thanks
""".format(booking.customer_name)

            print(email_body)
```

Let's try it out before looking into what the code does. Refresh the `changelist` page for the Booking model and look at the **Action** drop-down. It should have a new option, **Email customers**:

To test it out, select some booking objects from the list, select the **Email customer** action from the drop-down menu, and click on the **Go** button next to the drop-down. After the page loads, look at your console. You should see something similar to what's shown here:

```
Dear Jibran,
    We are pleased to inform you that your booking has been approved.
Thanks

[18/Jan/2016 09:58:05] "POST /admin/frontend/booking/ HTTP/1.1" 302 0
```

Let's look at what we've done here. As I said before, an admin action is just a method on the `ModelAdmin` class that accepts a `request` object and `queryset` as parameters, and then performs the required operation on `queryset`. Here, we create an e-mail body text for each booking object and print it to the console.

UX improvements

While the system is now good enough for our client to use, there is definitely room for improvement. For a start, the user isn't given any feedback whether the **Email customers** action was performed. Let's fix this first. Add this line to the end of the `email_customers` method:

```
self.message_user(request, 'Emails were send successfully')
```

Try using the e-mail action again. Now when the page reloads, you see a nice success message that assures the user that the action they wanted was completed. Small improvements in UX go a long way in helping the user navigate and successfully use your product.

Secondly, let's look at naming the action. For this action, Django comes up with a pretty good name—**Email customers**. It's simple and to the point. However, it's not as clear as it should be. It doesn't convey to the user what e-mail is being sent. In a larger system, the client could potentially send many types of e-mails, and our action name should be clear about which e-mail we are talking about.

In order to change the name of the admin action, we need to give the method an attribute called `short_description`. As methods are also objects in Python, this is pretty easy. Change the `BookingModelAdmin` class to match the following code. The new line to add is highlighted:

```
class BookingModelAdmin(admin.ModelAdmin):
    list_display = ['customer_name', 'booking_start_date', 'booking_
end_date', 'is_approved']
    list_filter = ['is_approved']
    list_editable = ['is_approved']
    search_fields = ['customer_name']

    actions = ['email_customers']

    def email_customers(self, request, queryset):
        for booking in queryset:
            if booking.is_approved:
                email_body = """Dear {},
We are pleased to inform you that your booking has been approved.
Thanks
""".format(booking.customer_name)
            else:
                email_body = """Dear {},
Unfortunately we do not have the capacity right now to accept your
booking.
Thanks
""".format(booking.customer_name)

            print(email_body)

        self.message_user(request, 'Emails were send successfully')
    email_customers.short_description = 'Send email about booking
status to customers'
```

Note that the new line (the last one) is not part of the function body. It's indented at the same level as the function definition and is actually part of the class rather than the function. Refresh the list page and take a look at the action drop-down again:

Delete selected bookings
Send email about booking status to customers

Summary

This chapter probably had the least amount of code written for any chapter in this book. However, the functionality that we built here is probably more complicated than what we built in most chapters. I said at the start of the chapter that one of the reasons for the popularity of the Django framework is the admin app. I hope that by now you agree with me.

With less than 20 lines of code, we were able to create a system that rivals most CMS systems out there and is still more tailored to our client's needs. Unlike most CMS systems, we don't treat Car and Booking objects as pages or nodes. In our system, they are first-class objects, each with its own fields and individual functionality. However, as far as the client is concerned, the admin works like it would for any CMS, probably easier, because there are no extra fields like there are in most CMS solutions.

We have barely begun to scratch the surface of customizing the admin. There are a lot of features provided by the admin, catering to most scenarios required by an administration panel. All of this power is easily available to use by changing a few settings on ModelAdmin. In all the Django applications that I have developed, I have needed to create a custom administration panel only once. The Django admin is so customizable that you just configure it to match what you need.

I highly recommend that you look at the documentation of the Django admin at https://docs.djangoproject.com/en/stable/ref/contrib/admin/. If you ever need to create an administration project for your web application, do check whether the admin provides the functionality that you want. More often than not, it does and saves you a ton of effort.

5
Multilingual Movie Database

The Internet might be the fastest growing phenomenon the world has seen. Cheap Internet-enabled mobile phones have accelerated this growth even further, and by some estimates, 40% of the world today has access to the Internet. Any web applications that we develop can truly be global. However, English users make up only around 30% of the Internet population. If your website is in English only, you are missing out on a huge audience.

To fix this, many efforts have been made in recent years to make websites accessible to non-English users as well. Django itself includes reliable methods to translate the content of your site into multiple languages.

However, translating the content is just the first part of the process. Language is not the only thing that is different between different parts of the world. Currency codes, time zones, and number formats are just a few examples. Adapting these to the location of your user is called **localization**. You will often see this abbreviated as **l10n**. That's the first l of localization, then a numeric 10, followed by the last n. The 10 refers to the number of characters between the two! You may also come across the term internationalization (**i18n**). Internationalization is making sure that your application works across multiple regions without errors. For instance, making sure any inputs that you accept from the user can be in a variety of languages, and not just the one you developed the app in.

In this chapter, we will make an application inspired by the amazingly useful **IMDB (Internet Movie Database)** website. If you have never heard of it, it's a web application that provides a lot of information about movies, both old and new. We will be creating an application that provides some very basic features similar to IMDB. As our application is multilingual (which IMDB is as well by the way), I will refer to it as the **Multilingual Movie Database (MMDB)**.

The code pack for this chapter includes a working non-localized copy of the application. Our job is to add localization and internationalization to it so that it works well for our users in France.

Requirements

Let's take a look at what we want to achieve by the end of this chapter:

- Getting an overview of all the features provided by Django to allow localization
- Translating the contents of the site into French
- Giving users the ability to choose which language they want to use the site in
- Persisting the language preference of the user across multiple visits
- Translating the content of models

Before we start, there is one thing I'd like to mention. As we are learning this stuff for the first time, we will start with an already existing Django application. However, our application is very small compared to most real-world projects. For larger applications, it is usually more difficult to add localization after finishing the project.

It is always a good idea to think about localization requirements when starting the project and then incorporating those features while developing the application for the first time, rather than doing so at a later stage when the application has been developed.

Getting the project up and running

As always, once you have downloaded the code drop, unzip it. Then, create a new virtual environment for this project and install Django. Finally, activate it and run the migrate command from in the project root. This should set up the database for the project and get you to a point where you can start the application. Now you need to create a new super user so that you can add some test data. From within the project root (with the virtual environment active), run the following command:

```
> python manage.py createsuperuser
```

Answer the questions and you'll have a new user. Now, run the application with the `runserver` command, then visit `http://127.0.0.1:8000/admin/`, and add a few movie detail objects to the database. Once you have added some test data, visit the home page for the application, and you should see something similar to the following screenshot:

You should take some time to explore the app. You can view details for a particular movie on a page, as shown in the following screenshot:

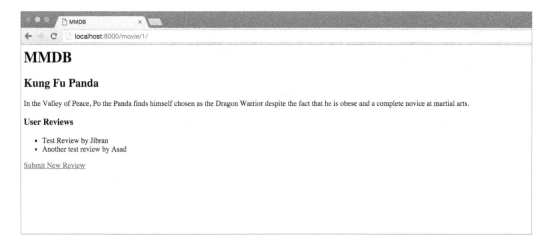

Finally, you can click on the **Submit New Review** link to get to the following page and create a new review for the movie, as shown in the following screenshot:

That's our entire application. For the rest of the chapter, we'll be looking into how to add l10n and i18n to this project. We'll be making very few, if any, changes to the core product features.

Translating our static content

The first thing that we want to do is translate all the static content on our site. This includes all the headlines, links, and form labels that you have seen in the preceding three screens. To translate strings that are used in templates, Django provides us with a `trans` template tag. Let's take a look at how to use it first in a simple context, and then I'll go into the details of how it works. This is a slightly long section as we will do a lot of things here that make up the foundation of the translation feature of Django.

Don't be alarmed if you don't understand something. Just keep following the instructions. I'll go into a lot of depth about each step, but first I want to show you exactly how translations are done.

Open up `main/templates/movies_list.html`, and replace `Movies List` in the `h2` tag with the following:

```
{% trans "Movies List" %}
```

Add the following `load` tag to the second line of the file, right after the `extends` tag:

```
{% load i18n %}
```

That's all the changes that we need to make to the template for now. I'll be explaining what these two lines do in just a little bit, but first I want to complete the whole translation process so that you can look at the whole thing instead of just smaller parts.

Next, let's run this command from the project root:

```
> python manage.py makemessages -l fr
CommandError: Unable to find a locale path to store translations for file
main/__init__.py
```

If you run this command, you should also see the same error as I did, something being unable to find a locale path. We'll explain what the locale path is after we're done with the demo. For now, create a new folder called `locale` in the `main` folder and run the command again:

```
>mkdir main/locale
> python manage.py makemessages -l fr
processing locale fr
```

This time the command succeeds. If you look in the locale folder that you created, you should see that a whole new hierarchy of folders has been created underneath it. What the `makemessages` command did was create a `django.po` at `main/locale/fr/LC_MESSAGES/django.po` file. If you open this file, you should be able to figure out a bit about its purpose. The last three lines of the file should be as follows:

```
#: main/templates/movies_list.html:5
msgid "Movies List"
msgstr ""
```

Together with the path of this file (`locale/fr/LC_MESSAGES/django.po`) and these three lines, you should be getting the idea that this file will contain the translated French text for the string that we marked earlier with the `trans` tag. Anything you put in quotes next to `msgstr` is what will replace the original string in the French translation of the site.

I used Google Translate to translate the `Movies List` string, and it gave me the translation as Liste des films. Put this translation in the quotes next to `msgstr`. The last three lines of the `django.po` file should now match the following:

```
#: main/templates/movies_list.html:5
msgid "Movies List"
msgstr "Liste des films"
```

Next, run this command from the project root:

```
> python manage.py compilemessages -l fr
processing file django.po in /Users/asadjb/Programming/Personal/
DjangoBluePrints/mmdb/mmdb/main/locale/fr/LC_MESSAGES
```

If you were to look in the `LC_MESSAGES` folder now, you should see that a new `django.mo` file has been created. This is the compiled version of our `django.po` file, the one that we put the translated strings into. For performance, Django translations require the file to be compiled into a binary format before it can pick up translations for strings.

Next, open up `mmdb/settings.py` and find the `MIDDLEWARE_CLASSES` list. Edit it so that the `django.middleware.locale.LocaleMiddleware` string appears between the already installed `SessionMiddleware` and `CommonMiddleware`. The position is important. The list should now look as follows:

```
MIDDLEWARE_CLASSES = [
    'django.middleware.security.SecurityMiddleware',
    'django.contrib.sessions.middleware.SessionMiddleware',
    'django.middleware.locale.LocaleMiddleware',
    'django.middleware.common.CommonMiddleware',
    'django.middleware.csrf.CsrfViewMiddleware',
    'django.contrib.auth.middleware.AuthenticationMiddleware',
    'django.contrib.auth.middleware.SessionAuthenticationMiddleware',
    'django.contrib.messages.middleware.MessageMiddleware',
    'django.middleware.clickjacking.XFrameOptionsMiddleware',
]
```

Next, add a LANGUAGES variable to the settings file and give it the following value:

```
LANGUAGES = (
    ('en', 'English'),
    ('fr', 'French')
)
```

By default, Django supports a much longer list of languages. For our project, we want to restrict the user to only these two options. That is what the LANGUAGES list does.

The last step is to modify the mmdb/urls.py file. First, import i18n_patterns from django.conf.urls.i18n. Next, change the urlpatterns variable so that the i18n_patterns function wraps all our URL definitions, as shown in the following code:

```
urlpatterns = i18n_patterns(
url(r'^$', MoviesListView.as_view(), name='movies-list'),
url(r'^movie/(?P<pk>\d+)/$', MovieDetailsView.as_view(), name='movie-details'),
url(r'^movie/(?P<movie_pk>\d+)/review/$', NewReviewView.as_view(), name='new-review'),

url(r'^admin/', admin.site.urls),
)
```

With this done, let's test and see what our hard work got us. First, open up http://127.0.0.1:8000. You should see the same home page as before, but if you pay attention to the address bar, you will notice that the browser is at http://127.0.0.1:8000/en/ instead of what we entered. We will look at the details of why this happens next, but in a nutshell, we opened the home page without specifying a language and Django redirected us to the default language for the site, which we specified earlier as English.

Change the URL to http://127.0.0.1:8000/fr/ and you should see the same home page again, but this time, the Movies List text should be replaced by what we said was its French translation, as shown in the following screenshot:

While all of this probably seems like a lot of work to translate a single sentence, remember that you only need to do this once. Let's see how easy it is to translate something else now that the foundation is there. Let's translate the word Stars to its French translation, Etoiles. Open up main/templates/movies_list.html and replace the word Stars with the following:

```
{% trans "Stars" %}
```

Next, run the makemessages command:

```
> python manage.py makemessages -l fr
```

Open the main/locale/fr/LC_MESSAGES/django.po file. You should see a new section for the Stars string that we marked for translation. Add the translation (Étoile) and save the file. Finally, run the compilemessages command:

```
> python manage.py compilemessages
```

Open the French language home page again by visiting http://127.0.0.1:8000/ fr/. You will see that the word Stars has been replaced by its French translation. The effort involved was minimal. The workflow that you just followed: marking one or more strings for translation, making messages, translating the new strings, and finally running compilemessages is one followed by most Django developers when they are translating a project. Most of the effort involved with getting a site translation ready is all the work that we did beforehand. Let's take a closer look at what exactly we have done to get our web application translatable.

How did all that work?

As I promised at the start of the previous section, after seeing Django translations in action, we will now take a deeper look into all the steps we followed to get to this point and what each of these steps did.

The first thing that we did was load the i18n template tags library, which provides us with a variety of template tags to translate content in the template. The most important, and probably the one that you will use the most, is the trans tag. The trans tag accepts a string argument and, depending on the language that is active, outputs the correct translation for that string. If the translation cannot be found, the original string is output instead.

Almost any string that you write in your templates will end up being wrapped by the `trans` tag and then later translated to the various languages that your web application is available in. There are certain situations in which the `trans` tag is not usable. For instance, if you have to add the value of some context variable to the translated string, the `trans` tag can't do this. For these cases, we need to use the block translation tag, `blocktrans`. We won't be needing it in our application, but you can read about it in the Django documentation at `https://docs.djangoproject.com/es/stable/topics/i18n/translation/#blocktrans-template-tag`.

Our next step was to run the `make messages` command. Our first attempt didn't succeed, so we had to create a `locale` directory in our `application` folder. Having done that, we ran the command and it created a message file with the `.po` extension. What the command does is it goes over every file in your project and extracts strings that you have marked for translation. One way to mark a string is to use the `trans` tag to wrap it. There are other ways as well that we will look at later.

After the `make messages` command has extracted the strings, it needs to create files and store the extracted strings in these files. There is a set of rules that Django follows when figuring out which file each extracted string goes to. For strings extracted from the files of an app, Django first tries to find a `locale` directory in the folder for that app. If it finds the folder, it creates the appropriate hierarchy underneath it (the `fr/LC_MESSAGES` directories) and places the messages file there.

If the `locale` folder is not found, Django looks at the value of the `LOCALE_PATHS` settings variable. This should be a list of directory locations. Django selects the first directory from this list of paths and puts the messages file there. In our case, we didn't have the `LOCALE_PATHS` setup, which is why Django raised an error, not finding a locale directory in our main application folder.

Let's talk a bit about the format of the messages file. Here is what our messages file looks like right now:

```
# SOME DESCRIPTIVE TITLE.
# Copyright (C) YEAR THE PACKAGE'S COPYRIGHT HOLDER
# This file is distributed under the same license as the PACKAGE
package.
# FIRST AUTHOR <EMAIL@ADDRESS>, YEAR.
#
#, fuzzy
msgid ""
msgstr ""
"Project-Id-Version: PACKAGE VERSION\n"
"Report-Msgid-Bugs-To: \n"
```

```
"POT-Creation-Date: 2016-02-15 21:25+0000\n"
"PO-Revision-Date: YEAR-MO-DA HO:MI+ZONE\n"
"Last-Translator: FULL NAME <EMAIL@ADDRESS>\n"
"Language-Team: LANGUAGE <LL@li.org>\n"
"Language: \n"
"MIME-Version: 1.0\n"
"Content-Type: text/plain; charset=UTF-8\n"
"Content-Transfer-Encoding: 8bit\n"
"Plural-Forms: nplurals=2; plural=(n > 1);\n"

#: main/templates/movies_list.html:6
msgid "Movies List"
msgstr "Liste des films"

#: main/templates/movies_list.html:10
msgid "Stars"
msgstr "Étoile"
```

Lines starting with # are comments. Then, there is an empty pair of msgid and msgstr. This is followed by some metadata about this messages file. After that, we get the main part of the time. A messages file, ignoring the metadata and first pair (the one preceded by the fuzzy comment), is just a list of msgid and msgstr pairs. The msgid pairs is the string that you have marked for translation, and msgstr is the translation for that string. The usual method of translating an app is by first marking all the strings for translation, then generating the messages file, and finally providing it to the translator. The translator then returns the file to you with the translations filled in. The benefit of using a simple text file is that the translator doesn't need to use any special software. If he has access to a simple text editor, he can translate the messages file.

Once we have translated the strings in the messages file, we need to run the compile messages command before Django is able to use the translations. The compile command, as mentioned earlier, converts the text messages file to a binary file. The binary file format is much quicker to read from for Django, and in projects with hundreds or thousands of translatable strings, these performance benefits add up very quickly. The output of the compile messages file is a .mo file in the same folder as the .po file.

Once we have our translations done and compiled, we need to set up a few Django configurations. The first thing we do is add `LocaleMiddleware` to the list of middlewares that our application uses. The job of `LocaleMiddleware` is to allow users to select the language of the site based on a couple of request parameters. You can read the details of how the language is determined in the documentation at `https://docs.djangoproject.com/es/stable/topics/i18n/ translation/#how-django-discovers-language-preference`. We will come back to it in a bit, discussing how it determines the language with an example.

We then needed to defined two settings variables, `LANGUAGES` and `LANGUAGE`. `LANGUAGE` was already defined in the code pack, so we only set the `LANGUAGES` variable. `LANGUAGES` is a list of language choices that Django can provide translations for the site in. By default, this is a huge list that includes all languages that Django can be translated into. However, for most projects, you want the user limited to a few languages to use the site in. By providing our own value for the `LANGUAGES` list, we ensure that Django doesn't serve pages for any languages other than the ones defined.

The `LANGAUGE` variable defines the default language to use. If you remember, when we opened the home page without any language code (`http://127.0.0.1:8000/`), the **English** language was selected by default. The `LANGUAGE` variable decides what the default language for the site is.

The next part of making the app translatable was to modify the `url.py` file. In place of the simple list of URL configuration elements, we wrapped our URL configurations inside of an `i18n_patterns` function. This function allows us to match URLs that have a language code prepended to them. For every request that comes in, this function tries to match the patterns that we wrapped in it after removing the language code from the URL path. It's a bit complicated to explain, so let's look at an example.

Let's say that we have the following URL pattern:

```
url(r'^example/$', View.as_view(), name='example')
```

This would match DOMAIN.COM/example/, but if we tried DOMAIN.com/en/ example/, the pattern would not result in a match as the /en/ part is not part of the regex. However, once we wrap it in `i18n_patterns`, it will match the second example. This is because the `i18n_patterns` function removes the language code and then tries to match the patterns that we wrapped in it.

In some applications, you don't want to have all the URLs matching with language prefixes. Some URLs, such as an API endpoint, don't change based on the language. In these cases, you can add together i18n_patterns and the normal list of URL patterns:

```
urlpatterns = i18n_patterns(url(r'^example/$', ExampleView.as_view(),
name='example')) + [url(r'^api/$', ApiView.as_view(), name='api')]
```

This way, you can create applications that are a mix of translated and non-translated views.

Having added i18n_urlpatterns, we are done with all the configuration that Django needs for basic internationalization, and we can visit the pages that we have in the French language and see the translated versions.

The last thing that I have left to explain is LocaleMiddleware. The locale middleware is the part of Django that allows users to use the language code in the url to decide which language to use. Thus, even though it's i18n_patterns that matches patterns based on language codes, it's the middleware that activates the correct language for each request. Other than using the language prefix in the URL path, LocaleMiddleware provides you with a few other ways to select the language as well:

- A session variable
- A cookie value
- The Accept-Language header that the user's browser sends
- If all else fails, the default language from the LANGUAGE setting variable is used

This is an overview of how we adapted our application to be translatable. However, we're not done yet.

Letting the user decide which language to use

While it's not a part of Django, almost all projects that are internationalized use this pattern; thus I think it's important that you are aware of it. Most sites that have multiple language options present the user with a menu to select which language they want to view the site in. Let's create that. Modify the `templates/base.html` template to match the following:

```
{% load i18n %}

<html>
<head>
<meta http-equiv="content-type" content="text/html; charset=utf-8" />

<title>MMDB</title>
</head>
<body>
<h1>MMDB</h1>
<div>
<span>Select Language</span>
<ul>
        {% get_available_languages as available_languages %}
        {% for lang_code, lang_name in available_languages %}
        {% language lang_code %}<li><a href="{% url "movies-list"
%}">{{ lang_name }}</a></li>{% endlanguage %}
        {% endfor %}
</ul>
</div>
    {% block content %}
    {% endblock %}
</body>
</html>
```

The new parts are highlighted. We first import the i18n template library. Then, we create a new `div` element to hold our list of language choices. Next, to get the language choices as part of the template, we use the `get_available_languages` template tag and assign the choices to the `available_languages` variable.

Next, we create a list of links based on the language choices. The return value of `get_available_languages` is the tuple that we set in the settings file for the LANGUAGES variable.

In our list of links, we need some way to get URLs for each language. Again, Django shines here, with deep integration between the internationalization features and the rest of the framework. If you have internationalization active and reverse a URL, it automatically gets the correct language prefix.

However, we can't just do a reverse for the URL here because that would create URLs for the language that is currently active. Thus, our list of links to switch language would actually just point to the current language. Instead, we have to temporarily switch to the language we want to create a link for and then generate the URL. We do this using the language tag. Between the language tag, the language that we pass as a parameter is activated. Thus, our reversed URLs turn out exactly like we want them.

One last thing to note is the URL that we reverse. For our application, the movies-list URL is the home page, thus we reverse that. For most applications, you'll do the same and reverse the home page URL so that switching the language takes the user to the home page in the specified language.

There are advanced ways by which you can keep the user on the current page and still switch the language. One is to generate the link on each page instead of base.html, as we have done here. This way, as you know which URL the template will be rendered for, you can reverse the appropriate URL. However, this has the drawback of requiring you to repeat yourself a lot. You can search on Google for Django reverse current URL in another language and get some other suggestions. I still haven't found a good one to use, but you can decide if you think one of the suggested options fits your needs.

Once you have made the changes, open the movies list page again by visiting http://127.0.0.1:8000/en/, and you should now see the language switcher links at the top. Refer to the following screenshot:

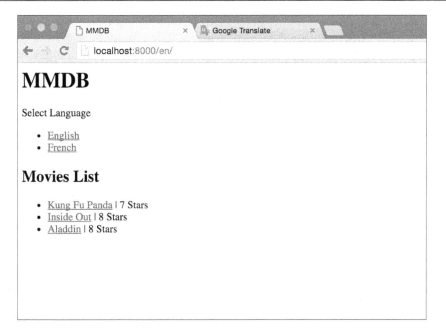

You can try switching the languages and see the change reflect immediately in the strings on the page.

Persisting the user choice

Let's try an experiment. Switch the language to French, and then close the browser window. Open the browser again and visit http://127.0.0.1:8000/. Note the absence of a language prefix in the URL. You will be redirected to the English language of the site. Wouldn't it be nice if, once you selected which language to use, it would persist across visits?

Django provides such a feature out of the box; you just have to add a few bits of code to use it. If you remember the list of steps that LocaleMiddleware takes to determine the language for the current request, the second step—after looking at the URL for a prefix—was to look at the session. If we can put the language choice in the session dictionary, Django will automatically choose the correct language for the user on subsequent visits.

What is the correct place to put the piece of code that updates the session dictionary? If you think about it, every time the user changes their language selection, we redirect them to the home page. As they will always visit the home page when their language preference changes, let's put our code there. Modify `MoviesListView` to match the following code:

```
class MoviesListView(ListView):
    model = MovieDetails
    template_name = 'movies_list.html'

    def get(self, request, *args, **kwargs):
        current_language = get_language()
        request.session[LANGUAGE_SESSION_KEY] = current_language

        return super(MoviesListView, self).get(request, *args,
    **kwargs)
```

You will also need to import `get_language` and `LANGUAGE_SESSION_KEY`. Put this at the top of `main/views.py`:

```
from django.utils.translation import LANGUAGE_SESSION_KEY
from django.utils.translation import get_language
```

Now, visit the site again and change your language to French. Next, close the browser window and open it up again. Open `http://127.0.0.1:8000/` and be careful not to put the language prefix in the URL, and you should be redirected to the French language page.

Let's look at what's happening here. In the absence of a language code in the URL, `LocaleMiddleware` looks at the session to see if the key that holds the language selection has any value. If it does, the middleware sets that as the language for the request. We put the language selection of the user in the session by first getting the language that is currently active using the `get_language` method and then putting it in the session. The key name used by the middleware is stored in the `LANGUAGE_SESSION_KEY` constant, so we use this to set the language selection.

With the session set properly, the next time your user visits the site without a language prefix, the middleware finds their choice in the session and uses that.

Translating our models

The last thing that we want to look at is how to translate our model data. Open the site and change to the French language. Your home page should be similar to the following screenshot:

You will notice that even though the static content — the one that we put in the template ourselves — is translated, the dynamic names of the movies are not. While this is acceptable for some sites, your model data should be translated as well in order to be truly internationalized. Django by default does not have any built-in method to achieve this, but it's pretty easy.

What I'm about to show you is something that the Django modeltranslation library already provides. I have used it in a large scale project and it works pretty well, so if you want to skip this section, you can just go ahead and use the library. However, it's nice to have an overview of how you can achieve it without any external help.

You can find the library at https://github.com/deschler/django-modeltranslation.

What we need is some way to store more than one language for each of the text fields in our models. You could come up with a scheme where you store both the English and French translation of the string in the same field using some separator, and then separate the two when displaying the model.

Another way to achieve the same result would be to add an extra field for each language. For our current example, that would mean adding an extra field for each field that we want to translate.

Both approaches have their pros and cons. The first one is difficult to maintain; as you add more than just one language to translate to, the data format becomes difficult to maintain.

The second approach adds database fields, something that may not always be possible. Plus, it requires a fundamental change in how to access the data. However, if you have the option, I always advice going with the option that results in cleaner and easy-to-understand code, which in this case means adding extra fields per language.

For our `MovieDetails` model, this means having an extra field each for the title and description fields to store the French translation. Edit your `main/models.py` file so that the `MovieDetails` model matches the following code:

```
class MovieDetails(models.Model):
    title = models.CharField(max_length=500)
    title_fr = models.CharField(max_length=500)

    description = models.TextField()
    description_fr = models.TextField()

    stars = models.PositiveSmallIntegerField()

    def __str__(self):
        return self.title
```

Next, create and run the migrations to add these new fields to the database:

```
> python manage.py makemigrations
You are trying to add a non-nullable field 'description_fr' to
moviedetails without a default; we can't do that (the database needs
something to populate existing rows).

Please select a fix:

 1) Provide a one-off default now (will be set on all existing rows)

 2) Quit, and let me add a default in models.py

Select an option: 1
```

```
Please enter the default value now, as valid Python

The datetime and django.utils.timezone modules are available, so you can
do e.g. timezone.now()

>>> ''

You are trying to add a non-nullable field 'title_fr' to moviedetails
without a default; we can't do that (the database needs something to
populate existing rows).

Please select a fix:

 1) Provide a one-off default now (will be set on all existing rows)

 2) Quit, and let me add a default in models.py

Select an option: 1

Please enter the default value now, as valid Python

The datetime and django.utils.timezone modules are available, so you can
do e.g. timezone.now()

>>> ''

Migrations for 'main':

  0002_auto_20160216_2300.py:

    - Add field description_fr to moviedetails

    - Add field title_fr to moviedetails

    - Alter field movie on moviereview
```

As you can see in the preceding CLI session, when I created the migrations, I was asked to provided a default value for the new fields. I just entered the empty string. We can fix the value later from the admin.

Finally, run the new migration:

```
> python manage.py migrate

Operations to perform:

  Apply all migrations: admin, contenttypes, main, auth, sessions

Running migrations:

  Rendering model states... DONE

  Applying main.0002_auto_20160216_2300... OK
```

Once this is done, open up the admin and see the edit page for one of the objects you have in your database. It should seem similar to the following screenshot:

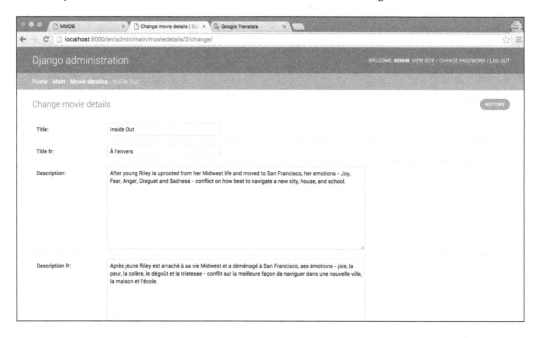

In the preceding screenshot, you can see that two new fields have been added to the admin. I translated the English value for these fields using Google Translate and filled in the French language field values. Click on **Save**. Now, our models have the French language data alongside the English values; but how to display them?

You could put a couple of `if/else` conditions in your template code to decide which language field to use. However, that gets messy quickly. Right now, our model only has two fields that are translated, but imagine a model with 10 such fields. How many conditions would you have? We're only talking about supporting one language. Finally, we only have two templates that need to be modified, the list view and detail view. In a real-world, more complicated application, your models could be used from a hundred different places. The `if/else` approach gets too difficult to maintain very quickly.

Instead, what we will do is give our model methods to intelligently return to us the correct value for a field, depending on the current language. Let's modify our `main/models.py` file again. First, import the `get_language` method at the top:

```
from django.utils.translation import get_language
```

Next, modify the `MovieDetails` model again and add these three new methods (highlighted in the code):

```python
class MovieDetails(models.Model):
    title = models.CharField(max_length=500)
    title_fr = models.CharField(max_length=500)

    description = models.TextField()
    description_fr = models.TextField()

    stars = models.PositiveSmallIntegerField()

    def get_title(self):
        return self._get_translated_field('title')

    def get_description(self):
        return self._get_translated_field('description')

    def _get_translated_field(self, field_name):
        original_field_name = field_name

        lang_code = get_language()

        if lang_code != 'en':
            field_name = '{}_{}'.format(field_name, lang_code)
        field_value = getattr(self, field_name)

        if field_value:
            return field_value
        else:
            return getattr(self, original_field_name)

    def __str__(self):
        return self.title
```

There's nothing Django-specific in the new methods. The main work-horse is the `_get_translated_field` method. Given a field name, it looks at the current language, and if the language is something other than English, appends the language code to the field name. It then gets the value for the new field name from the object. If the value is empty because we didn't translate the field, it follows the Django convention and just returns the value of the original non-translated field.

Now, modify `main/templates/movies_list.html` to use these new methods:

```
{% extends "base.html" %}
{% load i18n %}

{% block content %}
<h2>{% trans "Movies List" %}</h2>

<ul>
    {% for movie in object_list %}
<li><a href="{% url 'movie-details' pk=movie.pk %}">{{ movie.get_title
}}</a> | {{ movie.stars }} {% trans "Stars" %}</li>
    {% endfor %}
</ul>
{% endblock %}
```

The only change here is that instead of using the value of `movie.title` directly, we use `movie.get_title`. This is the one major drawback of this approach. Now everywhere in your project where you need the `title` or `description` values, you'll have to use the `get_title` and `get_description` methods instead of just using the field values directly.

The same goes for saving the fields. You'll have to figure out which field name to write to, depending on the active language. While neither of these are complicated, they do add some discomfort to the whole process. However, that's the price you pay for this power.

The `django-modeltranslation` package that I mentioned before has a good solution to this problem. It uses code in the model to automatically decides which language to return whenever you access any field. So, instead of using `obj.get_title()`, you would write `obj.title` and get the correct field for the currently activated language. For your projects, you might want to look into this. I didn't use this in this chapter because I wanted to give you a way to work with basic Django and show you one possible way to do things yourself instead of relying on third-party libraries.

Open up the French version of the site again and you should see that the one object we translated should have the translated version of the title, whereas the others will just show the non-translated versions:

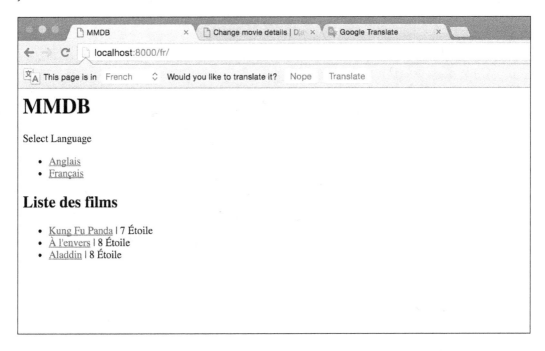

Doing the same for the details template should be simple and is left up to you!

Summary

While this was a somewhat small chapter, we looked at information that will come in handy throughout your web development career. While not all of the sites that you develop will need to be translated into multiple languages, some of the most important ones will. When you get a chance to work on such a project, you will have the information on how to go about creating a truly internationalized web application.

We have only scratched the surface of what is possible with Django internationalization and localization. When you start a project that requires these, be sure to check out the documentation as well.

We are now done with simple Django-only applications. Having learnt the basics of Django, the next chapter will have us working on a more complicated web application—one that involves search using the amazingly powerful Elasticsearch!

6
Daintree – an E-commerce Site

We have created some solid web applications in the previous chapters. They were simple, but had enough functionality to be used in real-world projects. With some frontend work, our applications could very well be deployed on the Internet and solve real problems. Now it's time to look at something more complicated.

I'm sure you have used, or at least heard of, some of the big names in the e-commerce space—names such as Amazon and Ali Baba. While these sites are very complicated beasts, a basic e-commerce site is pretty simple under the hood. E-commerce sites are also something that a lot of clients want created, so having some knowledge of how to make a good one will be very useful in your career.

A basic e-commerce site has one main purpose: to help users find and buy products from the online store. Django alone can be used to build an e-commerce site quickly, using database queries to allow searches across product range, but this doesn't scale well. Databases are designed to quickly save and retrieve rows of data, but they are not optimized to search across the entire dataset (or a subset). Once the traffic of your site starts to increase, you'll see the search speed go down very quickly. On top of that, there are some features that are very difficult to build with a database.

Instead, we will use a **search server**. A search server is very much like a database. You give it some data to store and then you can retrieve it later. It also has features specifically built to help you add searching to your applications. You might wonder that if a search server can store our data like a database, then can we not just get rid of the database? We can, but usually it's not recommended. Why? Well, because the search server is designed for a different use case. While it can store your data, a database provides a lot of guarantees about the storage that a search server usually doesn't. For example, a good database (such as MySQL or PostgreSQL) gives you a guarantee that if you try to save something and the database returns a successful response, your data will not be lost in case of a crash or power outage or some other problem. This is called durability. A search server does not provide this guarantee because that's not what they are designed for. It is usually a good idea to keep our data in a database and use the search server just to search across our data.

For the application that we will develop in this chapter, we will be using **Elasticsearch**, one of the most popular and perhaps easy-to-use search servers available. It's also open source and available for free. So let's get started. This is going to be an exciting chapter!

Code pack

The code pack for this chapter contains a basic web application that has the models and views for a simple e-commerce site. Right now there is no search, just a page that lists all the available products. I have also provided a data dump that contains about 1,000 products so that our database has some data that we can play around with. As always, download the code pack, create a new virtual environment, install Django, run the migrate command, and then issue the run server command to start the development server. You should have the hang of how to do these things without any guidance by now.

To load the test data, run the following command after the migrate command:

```
> python manage.py loaddata main/fixtures/initial.json
```

This should fill your database with a thousand sample products and give us enough data to play around with.

Exploring Elasticsearch

Before we get into integrating Elasticsearch with our Django application, let's take some time and explore Elasticsearch. We'll look into how to get data into it and use the search features to get back the results we want. We won't go into a lot of details about the search as we'll look into it later when we are building the search page for our applications, but we will get a basic overview of how Elasticsearch works and how it can be useful for us.

To start, download the latest version of Elasticsearch from `https://www.elastic.co/downloads/elasticsearch`. You will need to have Java installed on your system to run Elasticsearch, so go ahead and install that as well if you don't already have it. You can get Java from `https://java.com/en/download/`. Once you have downloaded Elasticsearch, extract the files from the compressed archive into a folder, open a new terminal session, and `cd` to this folder. Next, `cd` into the `bin` folder and run the following command:

```
> ./elasticsearch
.
.
.
[2016-03-06 17:53:53,091][INFO ][http                    ]
[Marvin Flumm] publish_address {127.0.0.1:9200}, bound_addresses
{[fe80::1]:9200}, {[::1]:9200}, {127.0.0.1:9200}
[2016-03-06 17:53:53,092][INFO ][node                    ] [Marvin
Flumm] started
[2016-03-06 17:53:53,121][INFO ][gateway                 ] [Marvin
Flumm] recovered [0] indices into cluster_state
```

Running the Elasticsearch binary should produce a lot of output, and it will be different from what I've pasted here. However, you should still see the two messages **started** and **recovered [0] indices into cluster_state** at the end of the output. This means that Elasticsearch is now running on your system. That wasn't so hard! Of course, running Elasticsearch in production is a bit different, and the Elasticsearch documentation provides a lot of information about how to deploy it for a couple of different use cases.

We only cover the basics of Elasticsearch in this chapter as our focus is on looking at the integration between Django and Elasticsearch, but if you ever find yourself stuck somewhere or need some questions answered, do take a look at the documentation—it really is quite extensive and thorough. You can find it at `https://www.elastic.co/guide/en/elasticsearch/reference/current/index.html`. There is also a book style guide available at `https://www.elastic.co/guide/en/elasticsearch/guide/current/index.html` if you want to really spend time learning Elasticsearch.

First steps with Elasticsearch

Now that we have Elasticsearch running, what can we do with it? Well, for starters, you need to know that Elasticsearch exposes its functionality over a simple HTTP API. So you don't need any special libraries to communicate with it. Most programming languages, including Python, include the means to make HTTP requests. However, there are a couple of libraries that provide another layer of abstraction over HTTP and make working with Elasticsearch easier. We'll get into those later.

For now, let's open up this URL in our browsers:

```
http://localhost:9200/?pretty
```

This should give you an output similar to this:

```
{
  "name" : "Marvin Flumm",
  "cluster_name" : "elasticsearch",
  "version" : {
    "number" : "2.2.0",
    "build_hash" : "8ff36d139e16f8720f2947ef62c8167a888992fe",
    "build_timestamp" : "2016-01-27T13:32:39Z",
    "build_snapshot" : false,
    "lucene_version" : "5.4.1"
  },
  "tagline" : "You Know, for Search"
}
```

While most of the values will be different, the structure of the response should roughly be the same. This simple test lets us know that Elasticsearch is working properly on our system.

Now we'll do a quick walkthrough where we insert, retrieve, and search for a couple of products. I won't go into a lot of details, but if you are interested, you should look at the documentation of Elasticsearch that I mentioned before.

You will need to have a working copy of the curl command-line utility installed on your machine to perform the steps in this section. It should be available by default on Linux and Unix platforms, including Mac OS X. If you're on Windows, you can get a copy from https://curl.haxx.se/download.html.

Open a new terminal window as our current one has Elasticsearch running in it. Next, type in the following:

```
> curl -XPUT http://localhost:9200/daintree/products/1 -d '{"name":
"Django Blueprints", "category": "Book", "price": 50, "tags":
["django", "python", "web applications"]}'
{"_index":"daintree","_type":"products","_id":"1","_version":1,"_shard
s":{"total":2,"successful":1,"failed":0},"created":true}
                                            > curl -XPUT http://
localhost:9200/daintree/products/2 -d '{"name": "Elasticsearch Guide",
"category": "Book", "price": 100, "tags": ["elasticsearch", "java",
"search"]}'
{"_index":"daintree","_type":"products","_id":"2","_version":1,"_shard
s":{"total":2,"successful":1,"failed":0},"created":true}
```

Most of the Elasticsearch APIs accept JSON objects. Here, we are asking Elasticsearch to PUT two documents, ids 1 and 2, in its storage. It may look complicated, but let me explain what's happening here.

In a database server, you have databases, tables, and rows. Your database is like a namespace where all of your tables live. Tables define the overall shape of the data that you want to store, and each row is one unit of that data. Elasticsearch has a slightly different way of working with data.

In place of a database, Elasticsearch has an index. Tables are called document types and live inside of indexes. Finally, the rows, or documents as Elasticsearch calls them, are stored inside of the document type. In our preceding example, we told Elasticsearch to PUT a document with Id **1** in the **products** document type, which lives in the **daintree** index. One thing that we didn't do here is define the document structure. That's because Elasticsearch doesn't require a set structure. It will dynamically update the structure of its tables (the document types) as you insert new documents.

Let's try retrieving the first document that we inserted. Run this command:

```
> curl -XGET 'http://localhost:9200/daintree/products/1?pretty=true'
{
  "_index" : "daintree",
  "_type" : "products",
  "_id" : "1",
  "_version" : 1,
  "found" : true,
  "_source" : {
    "name" : "Django Blueprints",
    "category" : "Book",
    "price" : 50,
```

```
        "tags" : [ "django", "python", "web applications" ]
    }
}
```

As you can probably guess, the API for Elasticsearch is very simple and intuitive. We used a PUT HTTP request when we wanted to insert a document. When we want to retrieve one, we use the GET HTTP request type and we give the same path that we used when inserting the document. We get back a bit more information than we inserted. Our document is in the _source field and the rest of the fields are metadata that Elasticsearch stores with each document.

Now we look at the star of the show — searching! Let's see how to do a simple search for books with the word Django in their title. Run the following command:

```
> curl -XGET 'http://localhost:9200/daintree/products/_
search?q=name:Django&pretty'
{
  "took" : 4,
  "timed_out" : false,
  "_shards" : {
    "total" : 5,
    "successful" : 5,
    "failed" : 0
  },
  "hits" : {
    "total" : 1,
    "max_score" : 0.19178301,
    "hits" : [ {
      "_index" : "daintree",
      "_type" : "products",
      "_id" : "1",
      "_score" : 0.19178301,
      "_source" : {
        "name" : "Django Blueprints",
        "category" : "Book",
        "price" : 50,
        "tags" : [ "django", "python", "web applications" ]
      }
    } ]
  }
}
```

The result is what you would have expected for this search. Elasticsearch only returned the one document that had the term Django in its name and skipped the other one. This is called the lite search or query-string search as our query is sent as part of the query string parameters. However, this method quickly gets difficult to use for complicated queries having multiple parameters. For those queries, Elasticsearch provides a full query DSL, which uses JSON to specify the query. Let's take a look how we could do this same search using the query DSL:

```
> curl -XGET 'http://localhost:9200/daintree/products/_search?pretty'
-d '{"query": {"match": {"name": "Django"}}}'
{
  "took" : 3,
  "timed_out" : false,
  "_shards" : {
    "total" : 5,
    "successful" : 5,
    "failed" : 0
  },
  "hits" : {
    "total" : 1,
    "max_score" : 0.19178301,
    "hits" : [ {
      "_index" : "daintree",
      "_type" : "products",
      "_id" : "1",
      "_score" : 0.19178301,
      "_source" : {
        "name" : "Django Blueprints",
        "category" : "Book",
        "price" : 50,
        "tags" : [ "django", "python", "web applications" ]
      }
    } ]
  }
}
```

This time, instead of passing a query parameter, we send a body with the GET request. The body is the JSON query that we wish to execute. I won't be explaining the query DSL because it has a lot of features and is quite powerful and it would take another book to explain it properly. In fact, a couple of books have been written that explain the DSL fully. However, for simple usages like this, you can guess easily what's happening. If you want further details, I will again suggest taking a look at the Elasticsearch documentation.

Searching from Python

Now that we have a basic understanding of how we can use Elasticsearch to insert and search on our documents, let's see how to do the same from Python. We could use the HTTP API of Elasticsearch from Python and query for the documents but there is a better way. There are a number of libraries that provide an abstraction over the HTTP API for Elasticsearch. Underneath, they are simply using the HTTP API, but the abstractions that they provide make it easier for us to communicate with Elasticsearch. The library that we will be using here is `elasticsearch_dsl`. Make sure that your virtual environment is activated, and install it using `pip`:

```
> pip install elasticsearch_dsl
```

Next, let's start a Django shell so that we can play around and figure out how to use it:

```
> python manage.py shell
> from elasticsearch_dsl import Search
> from elasticsearch_dsl.connections import connections
> connections.create_connection(hosts=['localhost:9200'])
<Elasticsearch([{u'host': u'localhost', u'port': 9200}])>
> Search(index='daintree').query('match', name='django').execute().
to_dict()
{u'_shards': {u'failed': 0, u'successful': 5, u'total': 5},
 u'hits': {u'hits': [{u'_id': u'1',
    u'_index': u'daintree',
    u'_score': 0.19178301,
    u'_source': {u'category': u'Book',
     u'name': u'Django Blueprints',
     u'price': 50,
     u'tags': [u'django', u'python', u'web applications']},
    u'_type': u'products'}],
  u'max_score': 0.19178301,
  u'total': 1},
 u'timed_out': False,
 u'took': 2}
```

Let's take a look at each line. The first two lines simply import the library. The third line is important. It uses the `create_connection` method to define a default connection. This is the connection that will be used whenever we try to do a search using this library with the default settings.

Next, we perform the search and print out the results. This is the important bit. This one line of code does a couple of things, so let's break it down. First, we construct a `Search` object, passing in the index name for the `daintree` index that we created earlier. As we don't pass in a custom Elasticsearch connection, it uses the default connection that we defined earlier.

Next, we use the `query` method on the `Search` object. The syntax for this is simple. The first argument is the name of the type of query that we want to use. As we did with `curl`, we are using the `match` query type. All other arguments to the query method need to be keyword arguments, which will be the elements of the query. Here, this generates the same query as our example earlier with `curl`:

```
{
    "query": {
        "match": {
            "name": "django"
        }
    }
}
```

Having added the query to the `Search` object, we need to explicitly execute it. This is done with the `execute` method. Finally, to see the response, we use the helper `to_dict` method on the response, which prints out whatever Elasticsearch responded with to our search; in this case, it is similar to what we got when using `curl` earlier.

Now that we have seen how to search, the next step would be to look at how to add data to our Elasticsearch index. Before we can do this, we need to learn about Elasticsearch mappings.

Mapping

I mentioned earlier that Elasticsearch doesn't require a data structure to be defined for the document types. However, Elasticsearch internally figures out the structure of the data that we insert. We have the ability to define this structure manually but don't necessarily need to. When Elasticsearch uses its own guess of the data structure, it's said to be using a dynamic mapping for the document type. Let's look at what Elasticsearch guessed for our `product` document type. Using the command line, make the following request with curl:

```
> curl 'http://localhost:9200/daintree/products/_mapping?pretty'
{
  "daintree" : {
    "mappings" : {
      "products" : {
```

```
        "properties" : {
          "category" : {
            "type" : "string"
          },
          "name" : {
            "type" : "string"
          },
          "price" : {
            "type" : "long"
          },
          "tags" : {
            "type" : "string"
          }
        }
      }
    }
  }
}
```

Elasticsearch has done a pretty good job of guessing our document structure. As you can see, it correctly guessed the type for all our fields. However, if you notice the type for the tags field, you'll see that it's a string. If you look at the document we retrieved earlier, the tags field is an array of strings. What's going on here?

Well, in Elasticsearch, an array doesn't have any special mapping. Each field can have one or more values; thus, each field can be an array without having to map it as such. One important implication of this is that arrays in Elasticsearch can only have one type of data. Thus, you can't have an array that contains both date values and strings. If you try to insert something like that, Elasticsearch will just go ahead and store the date as a string.

You might be wondering that if Elasticsearch is intelligent enough to figure out our data structure, then why do we care about the mapping? Well, the library we are using to work with Elasticsearch, elasticsearch_dsl, needs to define custom mappings to be able to insert documents into the index.

It is also a good idea to be explicit in what kind of data you will be inserting into the index. You can set a number of options when you set your own mapping, such as defining a field to be an integer. This way, even if you insert the value "123", Elasticsearch will convert it to an integer before inserting the document and raise an error if it can't. This provides data validation. There are certain types of data, such as dates in a format different than what Elasticsearch uses by default, that can only be correctly indexed if you have set a custom mapping.

Defining a mapping

To define a mapping with `elasticsearch_dsl`, we create a `DocType` subclass. This is similar to how a Django database model is defined. Create a new `main/es_docs.py` file and type in the following code:

```python
from elasticsearch_dsl import DocType
from elasticsearch_dsl import Long
from elasticsearch_dsl import String


class ESProduct(DocType):
    name = String(required=True)
    description = String()
    price = Long(required=True)

    category = String(required=True)
    tags = String(multi=True)

    class Meta:
        doc_type = 'products'
```

There shouldn't be any surprises here as the syntax is pretty self-explanatory. I prefer to add ES to the start of my document type classes to differentiate an ES doc type class from the Django model of the same name. Note that we explicitly specified the document type name. If we hadn't, `elasticsearch_dsl` would have automatically come up with a name based on the class name — `ESProduct`. However, as we just wanted to define a mapping for an existing document type, we set the `doc_type` attribute in the `Meta` class.

Notice that our data types are the same as the ones that we saw before when we asked Elasticsearch about the mapping. There is a reason for this. You can't change the data type for an existing field. Otherwise, the existing documents would have the wrong data type and the search would return inconsistent results. While this mapping already exists in our Elasticsearch, let's see how we would use this class to define a new document type mapping. Open up the Django shell again and type in the following:

```
> python manage.py shell
> from elasticsearch_dsl.connections import connections
> from main.es_docs import ESProduct
> connections.create_connection()
<Elasticsearch([{}])>
> ESProduct.init(index='daintree')
```

We use the `ESProduct.init(index='daintree')` method to create the mapping in Elasticsearch. As our mapping already existed and was exactly the same, this function didn't change anything. However, if we were creating a new mapping, this function would have configured Elasticsearch with the new document type.

Note that this time we didn't pass any parameters to the `connections.create_connection()` method, which means that it used the default host list that assumes a locally running instance of Elasticsearch on the default port of 9200. As our Elasticsearch is running locally on the same port, we can skip the host's argument to the `create_connection()` method.

Inserting documents into Elasticsearch from Python

Now that we have a `DocType` subclass and have seen how to create the mapping, all that's left to look at is inserting documents into Elasticsearch. This section assumes that you have loaded the fixtures data that I provided with the code drop.

Open the Django shell again and type the following commands:

```
> python manage.py shell
> from elasticsearch_dsl.connections import connections
> from main.es_docs import ESProduct
> from main.models import Product
> connections.create_connection()
<Elasticsearch([{}])>
> p = Product.objects.get(pk=200)
> esp = ESProduct(meta={'id':p.pk}, name=p.name, description=p.
description, price=p.price, category=p.category.name)
> for tag in p.tags.all():
>     esp.tags.append(tag.name)
>
> esp.save(index='daintree')
True
```

 Note the empty line after the for loop body. In the shell, this empty line is required to tell the interactive shell that the loop body is finished and it can go ahead and execute the loop.

It should be pretty normal, up to where we get the product with ID 200 from the database. I just chose a random ID as I knew that the product with ID 200 would exist in your database after you had loaded the fixtures I provided.

Next, we create a new ESProduct instance and assign it values from our Django model. The ID field needs to be assigned a value using the special meta keyword argument because that is part of the metadata of the document in Elasticsearch and not part of the document body. If we didn't provide an ID, Elasticsearch would automatically generate a random one for us. We specify it explicitly so that we can tie our database models to our Elasticsearch documents.

Next, we loop over all the tags in our Product object and append it to the tags field in our ESProduct object. We didn't need to set the tags field value to an empty array. When we defined the tags field, we passed the multi=True argument to the constructor. For elasticsearch_dsl fields, a multifield has a default empty value, which is an empty list. Thus, in our loop, we were sure that esp.tags is a list that we can append to.

After we have set up our ESProduct model instance with the correct values, we call the save method, passing the index name in which to insert it. Once the save call returns, Elasticsearch will hold our new data. We can test it using curl to retrieve this new document:

```
> curl 'http://localhost:9200/daintree/products/_search?pretty'
```

In the output for this command, you should now see three products instead of the two that we originally inserted.

Getting all our data into Elasticsearch

We can't go around inserting data into Elasticsearch from the console all the time. We need an automated way of doing so. As we've seen before, Django management commands are a perfect way to create a script to do so. Create the folders that will hold our command file, main/management/commands, create an empty __init__.py file in both main/management and main/management/commands, and add the following code to main/management/commands/index_all_data.py:

```python
import elasticsearch_dsl
import elasticsearch_dsl.connections

from django.core.management import BaseCommand

from main.models import Product
from main.es_docs import ESProduct


class Command(BaseCommand):
```

```
        help = "Index all data to Elasticsearch"

        def handle(self, *args, **options):
            elasticsearch_dsl.connections.connections.create_connection()

            for product in Product.objects.all():
                esp = ESProduct(meta={'id': product.pk}, name=product.
    name, description=product.description,
                                price=product.price, category=product.
    category.name)
                for tag in product.tags.all():
                    esp.tags.append(tag.name)

                esp.save(index='daintree')
```

There isn't anything new here. We just loop over all the product objects in our database and add them to Elasticsearch. Run it as follows:

```
> python manage.py index_all_data
```

It will run successfully without any output and you should now have all your documents in Elasticsearch. To confirm this, we can get the stats for our daintree index from Elasticsearch. Run the following command from your shell:

```
> curl 'localhost:9200/daintree/_stats?pretty=1'
```

This should output lots of data about the daintree index. You'll need to scroll up and you will find the total document count. It should be similar to this:

```
.

.

.

"total" : {
        "docs" : {
          "count" : 1000,
          "deleted" : 0
        },

.

.

.
```

As you can see, all our data is now indexed. Next, we will add search to our home page using Elasticsearch.

Adding search

If you look at our home page right now, it should be a list of 50 random products from our database. You can open it at `http://127.0.0.1:8000` and it should look similar to this:

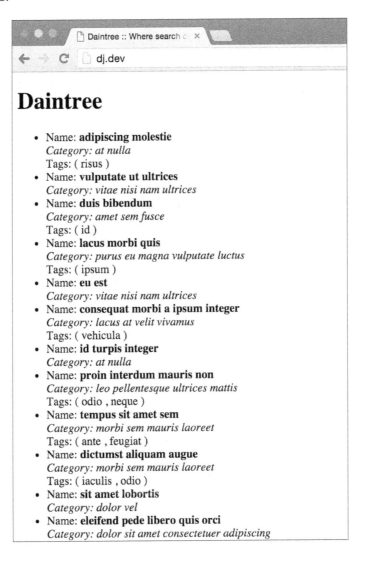

What we'd like to do is add a basic search form to this page. The form will just be one field that accepts a search term and button to perform the search. The search term will perform a search on the name field of our products list.

Let's create a simple Django form and add it to our page. Create a new `main/forms.py` file and add the following code:

```
from django import forms


class SearchForm(forms.Form):
    name = forms.CharField(required=False)
```

Next, we need to display our search form on the home page. Add the following to the `home.html` template, right after the opening tag of the `content` block:

```
<h2>Search</h2>
<form action="" method="get">
    {{ form.as_p }}
    <input type="submit" value="Search" />
</form>
```

Finally, we need to modify our `HomeView` so that it uses the user's query to generate the list of results instead of getting 50 random ones from the database. Change `main/view.py` to match the following code:

```
import random

from django.shortcuts import render
from django.template.response import RequestContext
from django.views.generic import View

from elasticsearch_dsl import Search
from elasticsearch_dsl.connections import connections

from main.forms import SearchForm


class HomeView(View):
    def get(self, request):
        form = SearchForm(request.GET)

        ctx = {
            "form": form
        }

        if form.is_valid():
            connections.create_connection()

            name_query = form.cleaned_data["name"]
```

```
            s = Search(index="daintree").query("match", name=name_
query)
            result = s.execute()

            ctx["products"] = result.hits

        return render(request, "home.html", ctx)
```

Let's test it first and then I'll explain what this code does. Enter a search term in the field and press the **Search** button. As our sample data has the usual Lorem Ipsum text in all the fields, search for a term like lorem. You should see something like this:

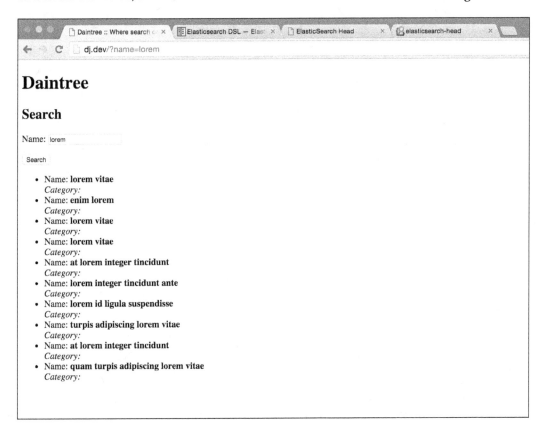

Try playing around with a few different search terms and see how it responds. If you enter something that is not found in our products list, you should see an empty page. We'll change it so that the user sees a message telling them that their search query has no results. Additionally, the category name has disappeared. This happened because the attribute name used in the `product.category.name` template is different from what our Elasticsearch document contains. While most of our field names in our Elasticsearch document were the same as those in our Django models, the category name needs to be accessed differently as it is no longer a foreign key but a simple string. In `main/templates/home.html`, note the following line:

```
<i>Category: {{ product.category.name }}</i> <br />
```

Change this to the following:

```
<i>Category: {{ product.category }}</i> <br />
```

The category name for our products will reappear.

If you experimented a bit, you'll notice that if you leave the field blank and click on the **Search** button, you don't get back any results. That's because if you give the match query an empty string to match with, it returns zero results. We can fix this by querying if the user specified a search term. Remove this line from the view code:

```
s = Search(index="daintree").query("match", name=name_query)
```

Replace it with the following if condition:

```
if name_query:
    s = Search(index="daintree").query("match", name=name_query)
else:
    s = Search(index="daintree")
```

This way, if the user didn't enter any query, we ask Elasticsearch to do a search with no query specified, and Elasticsearch just returns us the first ten documents that it has. This is similar to doing `Product.objects.all()[:10]` if we were using the database.

Now, let's change our template so that if there were no results, the user sees a nice message explaining that, instead of an empty page which the user might see as a bug in our application. Change the `{% for product in products %}` loop in our `main/templates/home.html` template and replace it with the following:

```
{% if products %}
    {% for product in products %}
    <li>
        Name: <b>{{ product.name }}</b> <br />
        <i>Category: {{ product.category.name }}</i> <br />
```

```
{% if product.tags.all %}
    Tags: (
    {% for tag in product.tags.all %}
        {{ tag.name }}
        {% if not forloop.last %}
        ,
        {% endif %}
    {% endfor %}
    )
    {% endif %}
</li>
{% endfor %}
{% else %}
No results found. Please try another search term
{% endif %}
```

Now if you enter a search term that doesn't have any results, you should see a message instead of an empty page.

The form and template code should be easy enough for you to understand by now. It's the view code that looks the most interesting. Let's take a look at the get method where all the magic happens:

```
def get(self, request):
    form = SearchForm(request.GET)

    ctx = {
        "form": form
    }

    if form.is_valid():
        connections.create_connection()

        name_query = form.cleaned_data.get("name")
        if name_query:
            s = Search(index="daintree").query("match", name=name_
query)
        else:
            s = Search(index="daintree")
        result = s.execute()

        ctx["products"] = result.hits

    return render(request, "home.html", ctx)
```

The first few lines simply instantiate the form with the GET params from the request. We also add it to our context dictionary that we later pass to our template. Then, we check whether the form is valid. If it is, we first use the `create_connection()` method from the `elasticsearch_dsl` library. We need to do this here because without this we would not be able to do a search later on.

 Some of you might say that this approach of configuring the connection to Elasticsearch in our view code feels like bad code. I agree! Later on, we'll fix this, don't worry.

After having set up our Elasticsearch connection, we check whether the user actually entered some search term. If they did, we then create the `Search` object and add our query to it. We specify that we need the `match` query type and we want to get documents where the `name` field has the query term entered by the user. In case the user didn't enter any search query, we need to set our search object, `s`, to a default search. As explained before, we did this because Elasticsearch returns an empty results list if the query term is empty.

Finally, we execute our search and store the results in the `result` variable. We then extract the results from the `hits` parameter of the `result` variable and assign it to the `products` key in our context dictionary.

At the end, we simply render the template using the context dictionary that we have prepared. As you can see, there isn't anything very complicated about using Elasticsearch with Django. The `elasticsearch_dsl` library especially makes this very simple.

Configuration management

In the previous code, we used the `connections.create_connection()` method to set up our Elasticsearch connection in the view code. This is a bad practice due to a couple of reasons. First, you have to remember to initialize the connection in every view where you want to use the Search object. Our example only has one view so we didn't run into this problem. However, imagine that you have three views that use Elasticsearch. Now your `create_connection()` method call has to be in all three of these as you never know which order the user will visit the website in and which view will be run first.

Secondly, and most importantly, if you ever need to change the way the connection is configured—maybe changing the address of the Elasticsearch server or setting some other connection parameters—you'll need to change it in all the places where you have initialized the connection.

Due to these reasons, it is always a good idea to have the code to initialize external connections in one place. Django provides us with a good way to do this using `AppConfig` objects.

When Django starts up, it will import all the applications listed in the `settings.INSTALLED_APPS` list. For each application, it will check whether the application's `__init__.py` has a `default_app_config` variable defined. This variable needs to be a string that holds the Python path to a subclass of the `AppConfig` class.

If the `default_app_config` variable is defined, Django will use the subclass pointed to as the configuration options for that app. If not, Django will create a generic `AppConfig` object and use this instead.

The `AppConfig` subclass has a couple of interesting uses, such as setting the verbose name for the application and getting the models defined in the application. For our case, the `AppConfig` subclass can define a `ready()` method that Django will call once when importing the application for the first time. We can set up our Elasticsearch connections here and then just use the `Search` objects throughout our application without needing to care about whether the connection was configured or not. Let's do this now.

First, edit the `main/apps.py` file and change the code to match this:

```
from __future__ import unicode_literals

from django.apps import AppConfig

from elasticsearch_dsl.connections import connections


class MainConfig(AppConfig):
    name = 'main'

    def ready(self):
        connections.create_connection()
```

Next, open up `main/__init__.py` and add the following line:

```
default_app_config = "main.apps.MainConfig"
```

Finally, from `main/views.py`, remove the import:

```
from elasticsearch_dsl.connections import connections
```

Remove the `connections.create_connection()` method call from the `get` method of the `HomeView`.

Open the home page again and do a couple of searches. You'll see that even without the `create_connection()` method call in our view, the search works fine. If you want to learn more about `AppConfig`, I suggest you look at the Django documentation at `https://docs.djangoproject.com/en/stable/ref/applications/`.

More search options

While our basic search is useful, our users will definitely need some way to search by price range as well. Let's take a look at how to add this to our search form. We'll use the `range` Elasticsearch query type to add this feature. First, let's change `main/forms.py` to add the two fields we'll need for this—minimum price and maximum price:

```python
from django import forms


class SearchForm(forms.Form):
    name = forms.CharField(required=False)
    min_price = forms.IntegerField(required=False, label="Minimum
Price")
    max_price = forms.IntegerField(required=False, label="Maximum
Price")
```

Next, change the `HomeView` code to accept and use these new fields in our search query:

```python
class HomeView(View):
    def get(self, request):
        form = SearchForm(request.GET)

        ctx = {
            "form": form
        }

        if form.is_valid():
            name_query = form.cleaned_data.get("name")
            if name_query:
                s = Search(index="daintree").query("match",
name=name_query)
            else:
                s = Search(index="daintree")

            min_price = form.cleaned_data.get("min_price")
```

```
max_price = form.cleaned_data.get("max_price")
if min_price is not None or max_price is not None:
    price_query = dict()

    if min_price is not None:
        price_query["gte"] = min_price

    if max_price is not None:
        price_query["lte"] = max_price

    s = s.query("range", price=price_query)

result = s.execute()

ctx["products"] = result.hits

return render(request, "home.html", ctx)
```

What we have done in the view is first checked whether the user provided us with a value for either the minimum price or maximum price. If the user didn't enter any values for either fields, there's no point in adding an empty query.

If the user entered values for either of the two price range fields, we first instantiate an empty dictionary (we'll look at why a dictionary is needed in a bit). Then, depending on which of the two price range fields the user entered data in, we add greater-than-or-equal-to and less-than-or-equal-to clauses to the dictionary. Finally, we add a range query, passing in the dictionary that we created as the value of the field name keyword argument, price in our case. Here is the relevant line of code:

```
s = s.query("range", price=price_query)
```

The reason we needed a dictionary here and not in the last example is because some Elasticsearch queries have more than just one option. In the case of a range query, Elasticsearch supports both gte and lte options. However, the library that we are using, elasticsearch_dsl, can accept only one parameter for any query type and this parameter needs to be passed as the keyword argument with the field name, price in our case. So we create a dictionary and then pass this to our range query.

You should now see the two fields on our home page and be able to query using them. You will notice that we give no feedback to the user about the price of the products. It's not displayed anywhere. So we have no way to confirm if the search is actually working. Let's add it now. Change main/templates/home.html to add this line right below where we display the product category:

```
<i>Price: {{ product.price }}</i> <br />
```

Now if you look at the home page, it will show you the prices for each product, and you'll feel that it provides a much better user experience as well. Plus, you can now test the minimum and maximum price search code as well. By now, our home page looks something like this:

Up to now, we haven't done anything with Elasticsearch that wouldn't have been just as easy with a database. We could have built all these queries using the Django ORM and it would work the same. Maybe we have gained some performance benefits, but at the small scale that our application operates at, these gains are almost negligible. Next, we will add a feature that would have been very difficult to create using just a database, and we'll see how Elasticsearch makes it so much easier.

Aggregations and filters

If you have ever used Amazon (or any other large e-commerce site), you might remember that on the left-hand side of the search results, these sites provide a list of filters that users can easily select and navigate the search results. These filters are generated dynamically based on what results are shown and selecting one further narrows down the search results. It's just easier to show what I mean with a screenshot. On Amazon, if you perform a search, you'll see something similar to this on the left-hand side of the screen:

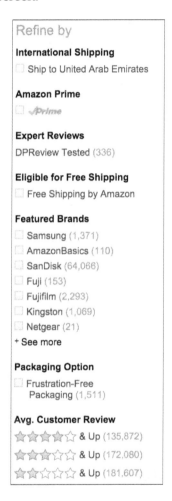

If you select any of the options listed here, you will further refine your search and see results relevant to only that option. They also provide the user with instant feedback, letting them know at a glance how many results they can expect to see if they select one of the available options.

We want to implement something similar in our application. Elasticsearch provides a feature called aggregations to help us do just this. Let's see what aggregations are first.

Aggregations provide a way to get statistics about our search results. There are two types of aggregations that can be used to get two different kinds of data about the search results: bucket aggregations and metric aggregations.

Bucket aggregations are like GROUP BY SQL queries. They gather documents into groups, or buckets, based on certain dimensions and calculate some metrics for each of these groups. The simplest aggregation is a terms aggregation. You give it a field name, and for each unique value of that field, Elasticsearch returns the count of documents where the field contains that value.

For example, let's say that you have five documents in your index:

```
{"name": "Book 1", "category": "web"}
{"name": "Book 2", "category": "django"}
{"name": "Book 3", "category": "java"}
{"name": "Book 4", "category": "web"}
{"name": "Book 5", "category": "django"}
```

If we run a terms aggregation on this data based on the category field, we will get back results that give us the count of books in each category: two in web, two in Django, and one in Java.

First, we will add aggregations for the categories in our products list and allow the user to filter their search based on these categories.

Category aggregation

The first step is to add an aggregation to our search object and pass the results from this aggregation to our template. Change HomeView in main/views.py to match the following code:

```
class HomeView(View):
    def get(self, request):
        form = SearchForm(request.GET)

        ctx = {
            "form": form
        }

        if form.is_valid():
            name_query = form.cleaned_data.get("name")
```

```
        if name_query:
            s = Search(index="daintree").query("match", name=name_
query)
        else:
            s = Search(index="daintree")

        min_price = form.cleaned_data.get("min_price")
        max_price = form.cleaned_data.get("max_price")
        if min_price is not None or max_price is not None:
            price_query = dict()

            if min_price is not None:
                price_query["gte"] = min_price

            if max_price is not None:
                price_query["lte"] = max_price

            s = s.query("range", price=price_query)

        # Add aggregations
        s.aggs.bucket("categories", "terms", field="category")

        result = s.execute()

        ctx["products"] = result.hits
        ctx["aggregations"] = result.aggregations

    return render(request, "home.html", ctx)
```

I have highlighted the new code, which is just two lines. The first line is as follows:

```
    s.aggs.bucket("categories", "terms", field="category")
```

This line adds a bucket type aggregation to our search object. In Elasticsearch, each aggregation needs a name and the aggregation results are associated with this name in the response. We give our aggregation the name, `categories`. The next parameter to the method is the type of aggregation that we want. As we want to count the number of documents for each distinct category term, we use the `terms` aggregation. As we'll see later on, Elasticsearch has a lot of different aggregation types that provide for almost all kinds of use cases that you can think of. After the second parameter, all keyword arguments are part of the aggregation definition. Each type of aggregation requires different parameters. The `terms` aggregation only needs the name of the field to aggregate on, which is `category` in our documents.

The next line is as follows:

```
ctx["aggregations"] = result.aggregations
```

This line adds the results from our aggregations to our template context, where we will use it to render in the template. The format of the aggregation results is similar to this:

```
{
    "categories": {
        "buckets": [
            {
                "key": "CATEGORY 1",
                "doc_count": 10
            },

            {
                "key": "CATEGORY 2",
                "doc_count": 50
            },

                .

                .

                .

        ]
    }
}
```

The top-level dictionary contains a key for each aggregation that we added, with the same name as the one we added it with. In our case, the name is categories. The value for each key is the result of that aggregation. For a bucket aggregation, like the terms one that we have used, the result is a list of buckets. Each bucket has a key, which is a distinct category name, and the number of documents that have this category.

Let's display this data in our template first. Change main/templates/home.html to match the following code:

```
{% extends "base.html" %}

{% block content %}
<h2>Search</h2>
<form action="" method="get">
    {{ form.as_p }}
```

```
        <input type="submit" value="Search" />
    </form>

    {% if aggregations.categories.buckets %}
    <h2>Categories</h2>
    <ul>
    {% for bucket in aggregations.categories.buckets %}
        <li>{{ bucket.key }} ({{ bucket.doc_count }})</li>
    {% endfor %}
    </ul>
    {% endif %}

    <ul>
        {% if products %}
            {% for product in products %}
            <li>
                Name: <b>{{ product.name }}</b> <br />
                <i>Category: {{ product.category }}</i> <br />
                <i>Price: {{ product.price }}</i> <br />
                {% if product.tags.all %}
                    Tags: (
                    {% for tag in product.tags.all %}
                        {{ tag.name }}
                        {% if not forloop.last %}

                        ,
                        {% endif %}
                    {% endfor %}
                    )
                {% endif %}
            </li>
            {% endfor %}
        {% else %}
            No results found. Please try another search term
        {% endif %}
    </ul>
    {% endblock %}
```

Again, I have highlighted the new code. Having seen the format of the preceding output, this new code should be simple for you to understand. We just loop over each bucket item and display the name of the category and number of documents having that category here.

Let's take a look at the results. Open up the home page in your browser and perform a search; you should see something similar to this:

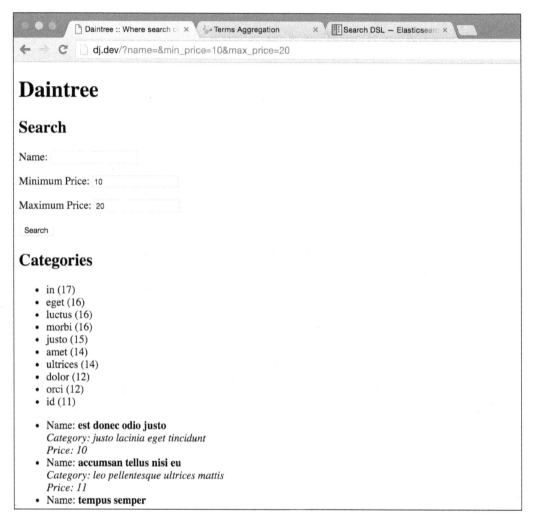

We now have a list of categories displayed. But wait, what's this? If you look closer, you'll see that none of the category names make sense (outside of the fact that they are in Latin). None of the categories that we see match what the categories our products have. How come?

What's happened here is that Elasticsearch took our list of categories, broke them up into individual words, and then ran the aggregation. For example, if three products had categories *web development*, *django development*, and *web applications*, this aggregation would have given us the following results:

- web (2)
- development (2)
- django (1)
- applications (1)

However, this is not useful for our use case. Our category names should be treated as a unit and not broken up into individual words. Also, we never asked Elasticsearch to do any such thing when we were indexing our data. So what happened? To understand this, we need to understand how Elasticsearch works with textual data.

Full text search and analysis

Elasticsearch is based on Lucene, which is a very powerful library to create full text search applications. Full text search is a bit like using Google on your own documents. You must have used the Find functionality in word processors such as Microsoft Word or on web pages a couple of times in your life. This approach to search is called exact matching. For example, you have a piece of text like this one taken from the preface to *Stories from The Arabian Nights*:

> *Scheherazadè, the heroine of the Thousand and one Nights, ranks among the great story-tellers of the world much as does Penelope among the weavers. Procrastination was the basis of her art; for though the task she accomplished was splendid and memorable, it is rather in the quantity than the quality of her invention – in the long spun-out performance of what could have been done far more shortly – that she becomes a figure of dramatic interest.*

If you search for the term `memorable quantity` using exact matching, it will not show any results. That's because the exact term "memorable quantity" is not found in this text.

A full text search, however, would return you this text because even though the exact term `memorable quantity` is not seen anywhere in the text, the two words `memorable` and `quantity` do appear in the text. Even if you search for something like `memorable Django`, this text would still be returned because the word `memorable` is still present in the text, even though `Django` is not. This is how most users expect search to work on the web, especially on e-commerce sites.

If you are searching for `Django web development` books on our site and we do not have something with the exact title, but we do have a book called `Django Blueprints`, the user will expect to see that in the search results.

This is what Elasticsearch does when you use a full text search. It breaks up your search term into words, and then uses these to find search results that have these terms in them. However, to do this, Elasticsearch also needs to break up your document when you index them so that it can do the search faster later on. This process is called analyzing the document and happens at index time for all string fields by default.

This is the reason why when we get the aggregations for our category field, we get individual words instead of the complete category names in the result. While full text search is very useful in most cases of search, for example, the name query search that we have, in cases like category names it actually gives us unexpected results.

As I've mentioned before, the analysis process that leads to Elasticsearch breaking up (tokenization is the technical term for this) is done at indexing time. In order to make sure that our category names are not analyzed, we need to change our `ESProduct` `DocType` subclass and reindex all our data.

First, let's change our `ESProduct` class in `main/es_docs.py`. Note the following line:

```
category = String(required=True)
```

Change this to be as follows:

```
category = String(required=True, index="not_analyzed")
```

However, if we now try to update the mapping, we will run into a problem. Elasticsearch can only create a mapping for fields, not update them. This is because if we were allowed to change the mapping of a field after we have some data in our index, the old data might not make sense anymore with the new mapping.

To delete our existing Elasticsearch index, run the following command in the command line:

```
> curl -XDELETE 'localhost:9200/daintree'
{"acknowledged":true}
```

Next, we want to create our new index and add the `ESProduct` mapping. We could do what we did before and create the index from the Python shell. Instead, let's modify our `index_all_data` command to automatically create the index when it is run. Change the code in `main/management/commands/index_all_data.py` to match the following:

```
import elasticsearch_dsl
```

```
import elasticsearch_dsl.connections

from django.core.management import BaseCommand

from main.models import Product
from main.es_docs import ESProduct


class Command(BaseCommand):
    help = "Index all data to Elasticsearch"

    def handle(self, *args, **options):
        elasticsearch_dsl.connections.connections.create_connection()
        ESProduct.init(index='daintree')

        for product in Product.objects.all():
            esp = ESProduct(meta={'id': product.pk}, name=product.
name, description=product.description,
                            price=product.price, category=product.
category.name)
            for tag in product.tags.all():
                esp.tags.append(tag.name)

            esp.save(index='daintree')
```

I have highlighted the change, which is just the addition of a new line calling the
`ESProduct.init` method. Finally, let's run our command:

```
> python manage.py index_all_data
```

After running the command, let's make sure that our new mapping was inserted
correctly. Let's see what mapping Elasticsearch has now by running the following in
the command line:

```
> curl "localhost:9200/_mapping?pretty=1"
{
  "daintree" : {
    "mappings" : {
      "products" : {
        "properties" : {
          "category" : {
            "type" : "string",
            "index" : "not_analyzed"
          },
          "description" : {
            "type" : "string"
```

```
                },
                "name" : {
                    "type" : "string"
                },
                "price" : {
                    "type" : "long"
                },
                "tags" : {
                    "type" : "string"
                }
            }
        }
    }
}
```

If you look at the mapping for the `category` field, it is now not analyzed. Let's try that last search again and see if this fixes our category aggregations issue. You should now see something similar to this:

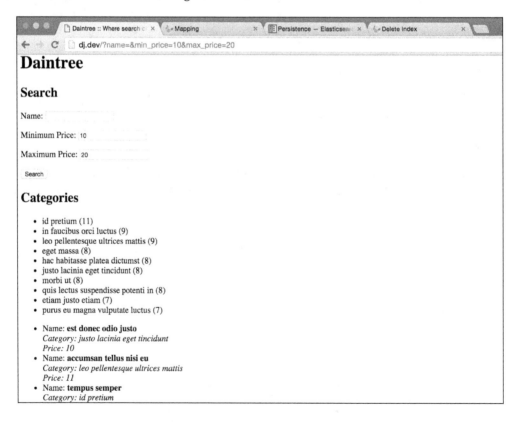

As you can see, we no longer have our category names split up into individual words. Instead, we get a list of unique category names, which is what we wanted from the start. Now let's give our users the ability to select one of these categories to limit their search to just the selected category.

Searching with aggregations

The user interaction that we would like to have is this: the user opens the search page or does a search and sees the list of category links. The user then clicks on one of those links and sees only products from those categories, with the user's previous search applied. So if the user searched for products with price between 100 and 200 and then clicked on one of the category links, the new search should show only products from that category while still applying the price filtering.

In order to achieve this, we need a way to create the category links so that the current search is preserved. We can pass the category to HomeView as another GET parameter. So we need to take the current GET parameters (which make up the current search) and add our category name to the end of it as another parameter.

Unfortunately, Django does not have a built-in way to achieve this. There are a number of solutions. You could build a custom template tag that adds parameters to the end of the current URL or you could use some if conditions in your template to add the category name to the end of the URL. There is another method, which I prefer because it is cleaner. Instead of generating the URLs in the template, we will generate them in the Python code where we have a lot of utilities to handle URL GET parameters and just pass the list of categories along with the URLs to the template to display.

Let's change the code for main/views.py to match the following:

```python
import random

from django.core.urlresolvers import reverse
from django.shortcuts import render
from django.template.response import RequestContext
from django.views.generic import View
from elasticsearch_dsl import Search
from elasticsearch_dsl.connections import connections

from main.forms import SearchForm


class HomeView(View):
    def get(self, request):
```

```
        form = SearchForm(request.GET)

        ctx = {
            "form": form
        }

        if form.is_valid():
            name_query = form.cleaned_data.get("name")
            if name_query:
                s = Search(index="daintree").query("match", name=name_
query)
            else:
                s = Search(index="daintree")

            min_price = form.cleaned_data.get("min_price")
            max_price = form.cleaned_data.get("max_price")
            if min_price is not None or max_price is not None:
                price_query = dict()

                if min_price is not None:
                    price_query["gte"] = min_price

                if max_price is not None:
                    price_query["lte"] = max_price

                s = s.query("range", price=price_query)

            # Add aggregations
            s.aggs.bucket("categories", "terms", field="category")

            if request.GET.get("category"):
                s = s.query("match", category=request.GET["category"])

            result = s.execute()

            ctx["products"] = result.hits

            category_aggregations = list()
            for bucket in result.aggregations.categories.buckets:
                category_name = bucket.key
                doc_count = bucket.doc_count

                category_url_params = request.GET.copy()
```

```
            category_url_params["category"] = category_name
            category_url = "{}?{}".format(reverse("home"),
    category_url_params.urlencode())

            category_aggregations.append({
                "name": category_name,
                "doc_count": doc_count,
                "url": category_url
            })

        ctx["category_aggs"] = category_aggregations

    return render(request, "home.html", ctx)
```

I have highlighted the new code that we have added. To start, we imported the `reverse` method from Django. Next, while making our search query, we check whether the user has selected a category (by looking at the category query param). If the user did select something, we add it to our search as a `match` query on the category field.

The more important part comes next, where we build the URLs for the category links. We loop over each of the buckets that we got in the aggregation results. For each bucket, we extract the category name and document count. Then, we make a copy of the request GET params. We make a copy because we want to modify the parameters by adding our category name in there, but `request.GET dict` is immutable and cannot be changed. If you try to change something in `request.GET`, you will get an exception. So we make a copy and add the category name for the current bucket in there.

Next, we create a URL for the request that will search using this category. This URL is made by first reversing the home page URL and then adding the query parameters — the one that we made by copying the current request params and adding our category name.

Finally, we add all this information to a list that we pass to the template. Our template needs to change as well to work with this new data format. Here is the new code for `main/templates/home.html`:

```
{% extends "base.html" %}

{% block content %}
<h2>Search</h2>
<form action="" method="get">
    {{ form.as_p }}
    <input type="submit" value="Search" />
```

```
</form>

{% if category_aggs %}
<h2>Categories</h2>
<ul>
{% for agg in category_aggs %}
    <li>
        <a href="{{ agg.url }}">{{ agg.name }}</a> ({{ agg.doc_count
}})
    </li>
{% endfor %}
</ul>
{% endif %}


<h2>Results</h2>
<ul>
    {% if products %}
        {% for product in products %}
        <li>
            Name: <b>{{ product.name }}</b> <br />
            <i>Category: {{ product.category }}</i> <br />
            <i>Price: {{ product.price }}</i> <br />
            {% if product.tags.all %}
                Tags: (
                {% for tag in product.tags.all %}
                    {{ tag.name }}
                    {% if not forloop.last %}
                    ,
                    {% endif %}
                {% endfor %}
                )
            {% endif %}
        </li>
        {% endfor %}
    {% else %}
        No results found. Please try another search term
    {% endif %}
</ul>
{% endblock %}
```

I have highlighted the code changes. It should be clear what we did here given how we have now formatted our category filters. One small change that is not relevant is the addition of the `<h2> Results </h2>`. That's because I forgot to add it earlier and only later realized that there was no divider between the aggregation filters and results. So I added that here.

You should go ahead and try playing around with the category filters. Select one of the shown categories and you should only see products from that category. Your screen should look similar to this:

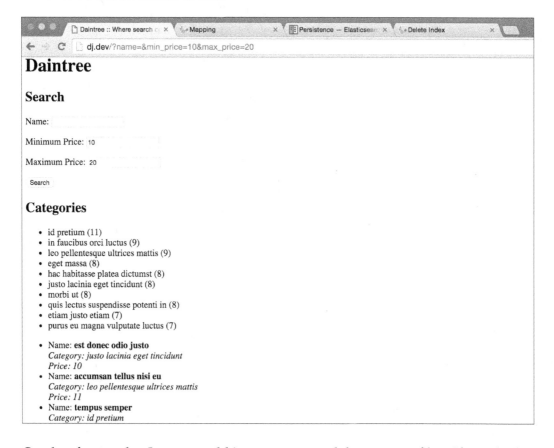

One last feature that I want to add is a way to cancel the category filter. If you think about it, we just need to remove the category query param to cancel a category filter, which would leave us with the original query that only included the search form params. Doing this is pretty simple; let's take a look.

In `main/views.py,` right before the `render()` call in the `get()` `HomeView` method, add this code:

```
if "category" in request.GET:
    remove_category_search_params = request.GET.copy()
    del remove_category_search_params["category"]
    remove_category_url = "{}?{}".format(reverse("home"), remove_
category_search_params.urlencode())
    ctx["remove_category_url"] = remove_category_url
```

In `main/templates/home.html,` add this right after the categories `ul` tag ends:

```
{% if remove_category_url %}
<a href="{{ remove_category_url }}">Remove Category Filter</a>
{% endif %}
```

That's it. Try using the search now, and select a category. You should see a **Remove Category Filter** link that you can use to remove any category search terms. It should look similar to this:

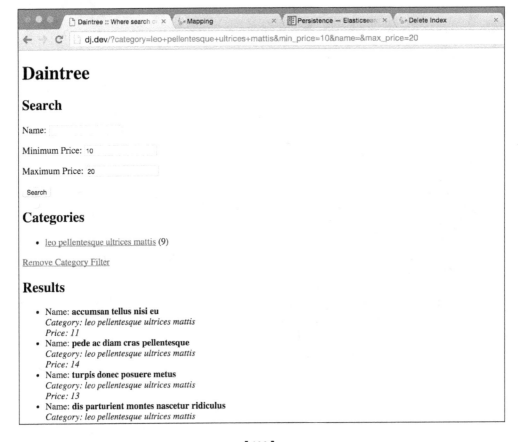

One thing that you might have noticed is that when any category is selected, we no longer see the other categories. That's because Elasticsearch aggregations are, by default, scoped to the main query. Thus, any terms aggregation will only count documents that are already present in the results of the main query. When the search includes a category query, the categories aggregation we have will only be able to find documents in the selected category. To change this behavior and show all categories, regardless of what is selected by the user, is beyond the scope of the book. However, I will point you in the right direction, and with some work, you should be able to achieve this yourself. Have a look at `https://www.elastic.co/guide/en/elasticsearch/guide/current/_scoping_aggregations.html`.

Summary

Wow! This was a pretty heavy chapter. We looked at a lot of things and gained a lot of knowledge. Especially where Elasticsearch was concerned, we went from 0-60 pretty quickly, having it set up and running searches within the first 10 pages.

However, I am confident that by now you should be able to pick up complicated concepts with ease. We first looked at how to get Elasticsearch up and running on our local systems. Then we looked at how we could easily interact with Elaticsearch using its HTTP API. We looked at the basic concepts for Elasticsearch and then inserted a few documents into our first index.

Then we used the HTTP API to search for those documents and get back results. Once we had an overview of what Elasticsearch was and how it worked, we moved toward integrating it with our Django applications.

We again saw the power of using the Django shell to test out libraries quickly and find out how to approach various tasks, as we did while indexing and searching for documents using the `elasticsearch_dsl` library. We then created a Django command that essentially was just a copy of whatever we did in the Django shell before.

Then we really started working on our search view. We changed the home page to use Elasticsearch instead of the database to show our products and added a basic search for the name field. Next, we looked at how to manage configuration options for our applications from a central location, `AppConfig`. We also looked at how to use `elasticsearch_dsl` to do a bit more complicated query, the range query.

Finally, we looked at what Elasticsearch aggregations were and how we could integrate them into our application to provide our users with a great search experience. All in all, this was a complicated chapter and having finished it, you should now have the confidence to approach much larger and feature-rich applications.

7
Form Mason – a Monkey of your own

In our journey to learn Django, we have traveled far. We started from baby steps, learning to set up databases, basic views, and templates. We then moved on to more difficult stuff such as management commands and the Django shell. This is the last chapter in that journey, where we use all the knowledge that we have gained, and use it to create one of the most complicated applications yet. It's always fun to end things with a bang, and that's what we'll do here!

You might have heard of SurveyMonkey (`www.surveymonkey.com`) or Wufoo (`www.wufoo.com`). If not, these are web applications that allow you to create custom forms to gather data from audiences. You use the control panel available on these sites to set up a form, defining all the fields and how they should be validated, and configuring some basic stuff such as what the form should look like, what theme it should use, and so on. After configuring the form, you get a link to a web page that displays that form.

You then send this link out to the intended audience and they fill it in, with their responses being saved. As part of your control panel, you also get a web page where you can view and filter these responses.

Services like these make it dead simple for even the least computer-savvy people to create online surveys and gather data for any purpose from a wide audience. This seems like a cool service that we will replicate in this chapter. It will also be the most complex application that we will have created, as it requires us to dive deep into Django and understand how Django forms work behind the scenes. In a sense, you will learn about the magic that makes Django tick. Exciting, isn't it!

Code pack

This chapter does not have a code pack because almost all of the stuff that we are about to do here is new. Plus, we will do a lot of exploring in this chapter as well. This is both fun and shows you one of the many ways of approaching a tough project.

As there is no code pack to work from, you'll need to start the project by yourself. First, as always, create a new virtual environment for the new project. Next, with the environment activated, install Django and run the following:

```
> django-admin.py startproject formmason
```

This should create a `formmason` folder with our new Django project, ready for us to start working on. Use the `cd` command to get into this folder and create a new application that we'll be using to hold our views, models, and so on:

```
> python manage.py startapp main
```

Finally, add the `main` application to our list of `INSTALLED_APPS` in `formmason/settings.py`. Once that's done, we're ready to start!

Looking at a Django form

As our aim is to allow users to create dynamic forms based on parameters stored in a database, a good place to start is to look at how a Django form works under the hood and what options we have to customize it. First, let's create a basic form. Create a new `main/forms.py` file and add the following code to it:

```
from django import forms

class SampleForm(forms.Form):
    name = forms.CharField()
    age = forms.IntegerField()
    address = forms.CharField(required=False)
    gender = forms.ChoiceField(choices=(('M', 'Male'), ('F',
'Female')))
```

This is a pretty basic form. However, it has a variety of form fields that we can look at. Let's play around a bit in the shell, which you can start as follows:

```
> python manage.py shell
```

I usually like to install another package called ipython. When you start the Django shell with ipython installed, you get an enhanced version of the basic shell with a lot of cool features such as autocomplete and a much better looking interface. I always install it in any Django project because I almost always use the shell at the start of the project to play around. I highly advise you to install it as well when you start a new Django project.

Import our form in the shell as follows:

```
> from main.forms import SampleForm
```

In the same shell, type the following:

```
> form = SampleForm()
> form.fields
OrderedDict([('name', <django.forms.fields.CharField at 0x10fc79510>),
             ('age', <django.forms.fields.IntegerField at
0x10fc79490>),
             ('address', <django.forms.fields.CharField at
0x10fc79090>),
             ('gender', <django.forms.fields.ChoiceField at
0x10fc792d0>)])
```

The first line of code simply created an instance of our form class. It's the second line where the fun begins. However, I'll first explain the `OrderedDict` data structure a bit.

As the name suggests, `OrderedDict` is a dictionary that maintains the order in which its elements were inserted. A normal dictionary in Python has no fixed order. If you insert three elements into a dictionary with keys A, B, and C, and then you ask for the keys back using the `keys()` method on the dictionary instance, the order in which you will get them back is not guaranteed, which is why normal built-in dictionaries are said to be unordered.

In contrast, the keys in `OrderedDict`, which is from the `collections` library (part of the Python standard library), are guaranteed to be in the same order that you inserted them in. So if you were to iterate over the keys using either the `keys()` or `items()` method, you would always get them back in the same order that you inserted them.

Getting back to the output, you will see that the dictionary printed has the same keys as the names of the fields that we used when we created our `SampleForm` class. The values of these keys are the `Field` subclasses (`CharField`, `IntegerField`, and so on) that we used in our form.

Let's try something. In the shell, type the following and look at the output:

```
> form.name
------------------------------------------------------------------
------
AttributeError                          Traceback (most recent call
last)
<ipython-input-16-1174e5d9164a> in <module>()
----> 1 form.name

AttributeError: 'SampleForm' object has no attribute 'name'
```

It seems that the `name` attribute that we defined on our `SampleForm` class is no longer there. Weird, huh?

So far you have learned two facts about a Django form. The first, that the `fields` attribute on a form instance contains a mapping of field names to the `Field` classes. Second, that the field attributes we defined when creating our `SampleForm` class are not accessible on the instance.

Putting these two facts together gives us some indication of what Django does with the `SampleForm` class when creating an instance of it. It removes the field attributes and adds them to the `fields` dictionary. After a form instance is created, the only way to find out the fields that are defined on it is the `fields` dictionary attribute.

So, if we wanted to add another field to a form after the class has been defined and we could not change the code of the class itself, we could add an instance of a `Field` subclass to the `fields` attribute on the form instance. Let's try it out and see if this works.

I lied a little when I said that Django removes the field attributes from a `SampleForm` class when creating an instance of it. In reality, the `SampleForm` class also has its field attributes removed. If you typed `SampleForm.name` in the shell, you would get a similar `AttributeError`. However, this information is not relevant to our current task, and the reason why this happens is complicated so I won't go into it in this book. If you want all the details, check out the source for the `django.forms.Form` class.

Adding an extra field to a SampleForm instance

We will now try an experiment. We will create an instance of our `SampleForm` with some valid test data, and then we will add another field to the `fields` attribute on our instance. We will then call the `is_valid()` method to see if our form instance considers the dynamically added field when validating the data provided earlier. Let's see what happens. In the Django shell, enter the following commands:

```
> from main.forms import SampleForm
> test_data = {'name': 'Jibran', 'age': 27, 'gender': 'M'}
> form = SampleForm(test_data)
> from django import forms
> form.fields['country'] = forms.CharField()
> form.is_valid()
False
> form.errors
{'country': [u'This field is required.']}
```

Nice! It seems like our idea worked. Even though we added the `country` field after our `SampleForm` had been instantiated and provided the data, the form validation did consider our new field. As the `country` field was not part of the `test_data` dictionary and the field is required, the form validation failed and the `errors` list included the appropriate error.

Now that we have a technique to achieve our objective, let's create some views and templates to render a dynamic form.

Generating dynamic forms

Before we get to the code, we have to decide on a data format to specify the structure of our dynamic forms. **JSON** is one of the most popular, if not the most popular, data storage and exchange formats on the web right now. You will probably be aware of what JSON, is and how it works and what it looks like. However, if you're not, here's a quick introduction.

JSON stands for JavaScript Object Notation. It uses the same format that JavaScript uses to declare objects. The biggest benefit for us Python guys is that it is almost exactly the same as the dictionary declaration syntax in Python. Let's say that we want to store some details about a user. In JSON, here is what that information would look like:

```
{
    "name": "Jibran",
    "age": 27,
    "country": "Pakistan"
}
```

As you can see, we can even copy and paste this into our Python code and it would be a valid dictionary definition, which makes it very easy for us to work with.

JSON has a number of benefits over other data storage/exchange formats:

- It's text only, so no need to have special tools built around it for the viewing and parsing.
- Parsing JSON is very easy, and most languages have a library for this. Python comes with a standard library to parse JSON.
- It's simple to write by hand.
- It can be stored in a number of ways without needing to do anything special. We will use this fact later on to store JSON in our database as a simple text field.

Now that you know a bit about JSON, let's see how to use it. We will store information about how to construct a dynamic form in JSON. We will then use the Python standard library json to convert the JSON string to a Python dictionary, which we will then iterate over and create our form.

 For this section, we will hardcode the JSON that we use in order to generate the form. Later on, we will allow our users to create and store the JSON themselves in a database from a control panel that we will make for them.

We will look at how to define the form fields in JSON and generate a dynamic form from this schema. We will also create an HTML form to render our form so we can test that everything works as expected.

Let's look at the format for a simple form that can be used to collect basic demographic information about people:

```
{
    "name": "string",
    "age": "number",
    "city": "string",
    "country": "string",
    "time_lived_in_current_city": "string"
}
```

This is the sample JSON that we will use in this section to generate and display our dynamic form. This structure is a simple dictionary with strings for the values. We have to write code to parse this dictionary and create a Django form out of this information.

Generating a form out of JSON

The first thing that we will need to do is convert the JSON data that our view will get to a Python dictionary so that we can iterate over it. Python comes with the json module as part of the standard library that will handle the parsing for us. You can read the documentation for it at https://docs.python.org/3/library/json. html. It is dead simple to use, however, so let's just dive in.

Open up main/views.py and add this code:

```
import json

from django import forms
from django.views.generic import FormView


class CustomFormView(FormView):
    template_name = "custom_form.html"

    def get_form(self):
        form_structure_json = """{
"name": "string",
"age": "number",
"city": "string",
"country": "string",
"time_lived_in_current_city": "string"
}"""
        form_structure = json.loads(form_structure_json)

        custom_form = forms.Form(**self.get_form_kwargs())
```

```
        for key, value in form_structure.items():
            field_class = self.get_field_class_from_type(value)
            if field_class is not None:
                custom_form.fields[key] = field_class()
            else:
                raise TypeError("Invalid field type {}".format(value))

        return custom_form

    def get_field_class_from_type(self, value_type):
        if value_type == "string":
            return forms.CharField
        elif value_type == "number":
            return forms.IntegerField
        else:
            return None
```

There are a couple of things to explain here. However, let's first get the view working and see if it does what we want. Then I'll explain what this code does. Next, let's create the `main/templates/custom_form.html` template. You will need to create the `templates` folder under the `main/` folder first. Put this code in there:

```
<html>
<head>
    <meta http-equiv="content-type" content="text/html; charset=utf-8"
/>

    <title>Custom Form Demo</title>
</head>

<body>
    <h1>Custom Form</h1>
    <form action="" method="post">{% csrf_token %}
        {{ form.as_p }}
        <input type="submit" value="Submit" />
    </form>
</body>
</html>
```

Finally, put the following code in `formmason/urls.py` to include our new view:

```
from django.conf.urls import url

from main.views import CustomFormView

urlpatterns = [
    url(r'^$', CustomFormView.as_view(), name='custom-form'),
]
```

That's it for now. To test it out, run the development server using the `runserver` command and then open up `http://127.0.0.1:8000` in any browser. You should see a screen similar to this:

Try submitting an incomplete form and the page should be rendered with the correct error messages. Try to complete the form and submit it. Now you should see an error page, with the `ImproperlyConfigured: No URL to redirect to. Provide a success_url` error. This error comes from our use of the `FormView` generic view. When the form is valid, it expects `success_url` to be defined so that the user can be redirected to it. We don't have anywhere to redirect the user to, so we will ignore this for now. Let's take a look at the code and see what we have done here.

This example also highlighted the power of generic views. By just redefining one function, `get_form`, we were able to use all the features of `FormView` with a form that is generated dynamically. As the Django generic views are made with modularity in mind, the rest of the view does not care how the form is created, just that the `get_form` method returns a valid form.

Most of the action happens in the `get_form` method of our `CustomFormView`, so let's start there. The first line of code defines the JSON data structure that we will use to generate our form. As I've mentioned before, this data will eventually be coming from a database backend; however, for testing purposes, we are hardcoding it for now. Next, we use the `json.loads` method to convert the JSON string to a Python object. This conversion process is pretty intuitive. The JSON string that we have is a dictionary with keys for `name`, `age`, `city`, `country`, and `time_lived_in_current_city`. The Python object that we get from `json.loads` is a dictionary as well, with the same key/value pairs. You can also have arrays in your JSON string and loading it would give you a Python list. JSON has support for nested objects, so you could have an array of dictionaries or a dictionary with an array for a value.

Next, we create an instance of the base `django.forms.Form` class. As we saw in our experimentation before, we can take an instance of a Django form and add fields to it. Instead of creating an empty form class and using that, we just use the base `Form` class from Django directly. To the constructor of the form class, we pass whatever we receive from `self.get_form_kwargs()`. This method is part of the Django `FormView` class and depending on the request type creates the correct keyword arguments to be passed to a `Form` class. For instance, if the request was a POST/PUT request, `get_form_kwargs()` would return a dictionary that contains the `data` keyword argument so that we can use the form to validate and take further action on the data.

The interesting bit happens next, when we loop over the items list of our custom fields data. The `items()` method on the data that we loaded from JSON returns a list as follows:

```
[('name', 'string'), ('age', 'number'), ('city', 'string'),
('country', 'string'), ('time_lived_in_city', 'string')]
```

We loop over this list, assigning each of these item pairs to variables `key` and `value` in the `for` loop. We then pass the values to the `get_field_class_from_type` method, which decides which of the available form field classes to use for the type of data passed. The method's code is a simple `if`/`else`, which returns a field class or `None` if it was passed an invalid type.

We use the return value of this method, which is a class, and assign an instance of it to the form's `fields` attribute dictionary. *Note that we assign an instance of the field class and not the class itself.* The name of the field is the key from our JSON dictionary. We also do some basic error handling, raising `TypeError` if we cannot find a matching field class for the type we got in our JSON data dictionary.

Finally, we return our customized form class. From there on, the Django `FormView` takes over and either renders the form, with errors if necessary, or redirects the user to the success URL if the form data submitted by the user was valid. As we didn't define any success URL, we get an error when we submit a valid form.

That's it. That is all the code that we need to create a dynamically generated form. We can add a couple of more features such as custom validation or advanced features such as supporting choice fields with a limited set of choices, but I'll leave that as an interesting project for you to try on your own.

Next, let's take a look at how we can store the JSON data that defines our custom form in a database. We'll create a model for it and allow the user to create multiple forms with different fields from an admin panel.

A model for our JSON

As I have mentioned earlier, one of the biggest benefits of using JSON as the definition format for our forms is that it uses just simple text data to encode the definition of complex objects. While some databases such as PostgreSQL have a column type for JSON, others do not. However, because we are dealing with simple text data, we don't need one! We can store our JSON data in a simple `TextField` and then encode and decode the data to and from a Python dictionary whenever required. In fact, there are many people in the Django community who have already dealt with this problem and open sourced their solutions for us to use.

One such package that I have used in the past is `django-jsonfield`. You can find it at `https://github.com/bradjasper/django-jsonfield`, and we will be using it in our project. First, install the required package by typing the following command in your command line. Make sure to have the virtual environment activated first so that it is installed in the correct location.

```
> pip install jsonfield
```

With the package installed, we can create a model for our form. Open up `main/models.py` and change it to have the following code:

```python
from __future__ import unicode_literals

from django.db import models

from jsonfield import JSONField


class FormSchema(models.Model):
    title = models.CharField(max_length=100)
    schema = JSONField()
```

Save the file and then create and run migrations so that Django creates the tables for our new model. In the command line, run the following commands:

```
> python manage.py makemigrations main
Migrations for 'main':
  0001_initial.py:
    - Create model FormSchema
> python manage.py migrate
Operations to perform:
  Apply all migrations: sessions, contenttypes, admin, main, auth
Running migrations:
  Rendering model states... DONE
  Applying contenttypes.0001_initial... OK
  Applying auth.0001_initial... OK
  Applying admin.0001_initial... OK
  Applying admin.0002_logentry_remove_auto_add... OK
  Applying contenttypes.0002_remove_content_type_name... OK
  Applying auth.0002_alter_permission_name_max_length... OK
  Applying auth.0003_alter_user_email_max_length... OK
  Applying auth.0004_alter_user_username_opts... OK
  Applying auth.0005_alter_user_last_login_null... OK
  Applying auth.0006_require_contenttypes_0002... OK
  Applying auth.0007_alter_validators_add_error_messages... OK
  Applying sessions.0001_initial... OK
```

With the migrations done, let's see how we can use this model. Instead of writing the code for the view, I like to start by doing a bit of experimentation in the Django shell. Open it up by typing as follows:

```
> python manage.py shell
```

Then type in the following to test out our new model:

```
> from main.models import FormSchema
> fs = FormSchema()
> fs.title = 'My First Form'
> fs.schema = {'name': 'string', 'age': 'number', 'city': 'string',
'country': 'string', 'time_lived_in_current_city': 'string'}
> fs.save()
> FormSchema.objects.get(pk=1).schema
{u'age': u'number',
 u'city': u'string',
 u'country': u'string',
 u'name': u'string',
 u'time_lived_in_current_city': u'string'}
```

What we have done here should be pretty simple for you to understand by now. The important thing to note here is the value that we assigned to the schema field. Instead of using a string representation of the JSON data, we simply assigned a Python dictionary to it. The JSONField class we used as the field class in our model does the heavy lifting of converting from a Python dictionary to a JSON string when saving to the database.

The reverse is also the same. Notice how, in the last line of our shell session, we simply accessed the schema field directly and got a Python dictionary back instead of the string JSON data that is actually saved in the database. This makes working with JSON transparent to us.

You might be wondering why I am asking you to experiment in this chapter and play around in the shell, whereas in the previous chapters, I just showed you the relevant view/model/template code directly.

Like I mentioned at the start of this chapter, this chapter is about showing you how to arrive at a solution by yourself instead of me holding your hand and showing you the end result immediately.

All good Django developers that I know have a similar method of developing solutions for the projects that they work on. They experiment a bit, and in doing so figure out a solution to the problem they are working on. Everyone has a different way of experimenting though. Some people, like me, use the Django shell a lot. Others write test code in views and models. Others might create simple Django management commands to do the same. However, everyone goes through the same process.

We find a problem that needs to be solved, we research it a bit, and then experiment with the various methods of solving it, finally choosing one which we like the best. You will eventually develop a method that you are comfortable with. In the meanwhile, I'll be walking you through my method and you can use this if you like.

We now have a `FormSchema` object in our database, so let's create a view that can use this object to generate a form. In `main/views.py`, first import our new model near the top:

```
from main.models import FormSchema
```

Then change the `get_form` method in our `CustomFormView` to match this:

```
def get_form(self):
    form_structure = FormSchema.objects.get(pk=1).schema

    custom_form = forms.Form(**self.get_form_kwargs())
    for key, value in form_structure.items():
        field_class = self.get_field_class_from_type(value)
        if field_class is not None:
            custom_form.fields[key] = field_class()
        else:
            raise TypeError("Invalid field type {}".format(value))

    return custom_form
```

I have highlighted the new line. We have removed the hardcoded JSON string that we used and instead assigned the `schema` field's value from our database object to the `form_structure` variable. The rest of the code stays the same. Try opening the home page for the application again. You'll find that the frontend has stayed the same. The interactions will be the same as well. You can try to submit invalid or incomplete data and it will show you the errors as before. Trying to submit a valid form will still result in the error about success URL not being defined.

Next, let's create a better frontend for our users. We'll create a list view where the user can see a list of all forms available on the site and a form view that displays the actual form and handles the interactions.

Creating a better user interface

There isn't anything complicated about what we'll do here. It should be very easy for you to follow along, so I'll just give you the code to write and leave the explanation, as we have done all of this many times before in the previous chapters.

Start by creating a `templates` directory in the project root. Next, add it to the list of `DIRS` in the `TEMPLATES` configuration variable in our `formmason/settings.py` file. The `settings.py` file already has a `TEMPLATES` variable configured, so go ahead and replace the `DIRS` list in this dictionary with the value that you see here:

```
TEMPLATES = [
    {
        'BACKEND': 'django.template.backends.django.DjangoTemplates',
        'DIRS': [
            os.path.join(BASE_DIR, 'templates'),
        ],
        'APP_DIRS': True,
        'OPTIONS': {
            'context_processors': [
                'django.template.context_processors.debug',
                'django.template.context_processors.request',
                'django.contrib.auth.context_processors.auth',
                'django.contrib.messages.context_processors.messages',
            ],
        },
    },
]
```

Next, create a `base.html` template in the new `templates` directory that you just created and put this code in there:

```
<html>
<head>
    <meta http-equiv="content-type" content="text/html; charset=utf-8"
/>

    <title>Form Mason</title>
</head>

<body>
    <a href="{% url 'home' %}">Home</a>
    {% block content %}
    {% endblock %}
</body>
</html>
```

Modify `main/templates/custom_form.html` to match this:

```
{% extends "base.html" %}

{% block content %}
    <h1>Custom Form</h1>
    <form action="" method="post">{% csrf_token %}
        {{ form.as_p }}
        <input type="submit" value="Submit" />
    </form>
{% endblock %}
```

Change `main/views.py` to this:

```
from django import forms
from django.views.generic import FormView
from django.views.generic import ListView

from main.models import FormSchema


class HomePageView(ListView):
    model = FormSchema
    template_name = "home.html"


class CustomFormView(FormView):
```

```
        template_name = "custom_form.html"

    def get_form(self):
        form_structure = FormSchema.objects.get(pk=self.kwargs["form_
pk"]).schema

        custom_form = forms.Form(**self.get_form_kwargs())
        for key, value in form_structure.items():
            field_class = self.get_field_class_from_type(value)
            if field_class is not None:
                custom_form.fields[key] = field_class()
            else:
                raise TypeError("Invalid field type {}".format(value))

        return custom_form

    def get_field_class_from_type(self, value_type):
        if value_type == "string":
            return forms.CharField
        elif value_type == "number":
            return forms.IntegerField
        else:
            return None
```

Create a new home template at `main/templates/home.html` and give it the
following code:

```
{% extends "base.html" %}

{% block content %}
    <h1>Available Forms</h1>
    {% if object_list %}
    <ul>
        {% for form in object_list %}
        <li><a href="{% url 'custom-form' form_pk=form.pk %}">{{ form.
title }}</a></li>
        {% endfor %}
    </ul>
    {% endif %}
{% endblock %}
```

Finally, change `formmason/urls.py` to match this:

```
from django.conf.urls import url

from main.views import CustomFormView
from main.views import HomePageView

urlpatterns = [
    url(r'^$', HomePageView.as_view(), name='home'),
    url(r'^form/(?P<form_pk>\d+)/$', CustomFormView.as_view(),
name='custom-form'),
]
```

Once you have done all this, open up the home page for the application again at `http://127.0.0.1:8000`, and you should see a page similar to this:

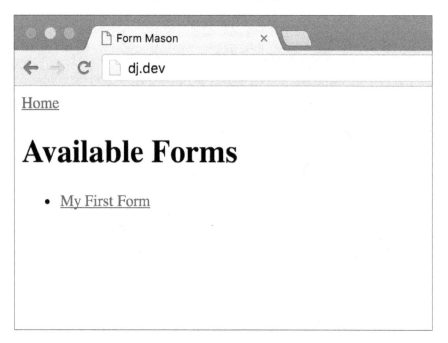

Clicking on the link for the form should take you to the same form page that we had before; the only difference is that now it is served at the URL, `http://127.0.0.1:8000/form/1/`.

Like I said, all this is pretty basic stuff that we have done repeatedly in the past few chapters. One thing that might be new is our use of `self.kwargs['form_pk']` in the `CustomFormView.get_form` method. Here's the relevant line:

```
form_structure = FormSchema.objects.get(pk=self.kwargs["form_pk"]).schema
```

For any generic view that Django provides (except for the base `View` class), `self.kwargs` is a dictionary of all named parameters that matched the URL pattern. If you look at our `formmason/urls.py` file, we defined the URL for our custom form page like this:

```
url(r'^form/(?P<form_pk>\d+)/$', CustomFormView.as_view(),
name='custom-form')
```

In our view, the `form_pk` parameter defined in the regex pattern for the URL is available in `self.kwargs`. Likewise, any non-keyword parameters in the URL pattern are available for use in `self.args`.

Now that we have a useable user interface, we will move on to storing the form responses in our database and giving our customers a page to view these responses.

Saving the responses

We want to save the response of the user filling in one of our dynamic forms. As the data from a dynamic form will also be dynamic, we need to store an unknown number of fields and their values in our database. As we have already seen, JSON is a reasonable way to store such data. Let's create a new model in `main/models.py` to store the responses:

```
class FormResponse(models.Model):
    form = models.ForeignKey(FormSchema)
    response = JSONField()
```

Next, create and run the migrations to add this new model to our database:

```
> python manage.py makemigrations main
Migrations for 'main':
  0002_formresponse.py:
    - Create model FormResponse
> python manage.py migrate main
Operations to perform:
  Apply all migrations: main
Running migrations:
  Rendering model states... DONE
  Applying main.0002_formresponse... OK
```

Now that we have our model, we need to save valid responses for our forms in this model. The `form_valid` method of `CustomFormView` is the correct place to add this logic. First, we need to import a few things from Django and our new model at the top of our `main/views.py` file:

```
from django.core.urlresolvers import reverse
from django.http.response import HttpResponseRedirect

from main.models import FormResponse
```

Then, add a `form_valid` method with this code to the `CustomFormView` class:

```
def form_valid(self, form):
    custom_form = FormSchema.objects.get(pk=self.kwargs["form_pk"])
    user_response = form.cleaned_data

    form_response = FormResponse(form=custom_form, response=user_
response)
    form_response.save()

    return HttpResponseRedirect(reverse('home'))
```

That's it. Now try submitting the custom form that we created earlier and if the data was valid, you should be redirected to the home page after your response was saved. Right now, we have no way to see these responses in the frontend; however, we can use the Django shell to make sure that our data has been saved. Start the shell with the following command:

```
> python manage.py shell
```

Then use the following lines of code to see the response that was saved:

```
> from main.models import FormResponse
> FormResponse.objects.all()[0].response
{u'age': 27,
 u'city': u'Dubai',
 u'country': u'UAE',
 u'name': u'Jibran',
 u'time_lived_in_current_city': u'3 years'}
```

You should see the data that you entered when saving the form. Now let's create a screen where our customers can see the responses for their custom forms.

Showing the responses

The code in this section is pretty simple and should not have any surprises for you.
First, let's create the view in `main/views.py`:

```python
class FormResponsesListView(ListView):
    template_name = "form_responses.html"

    def get_context_data(self, **kwargs):
        ctx = super(FormResponsesListView, self).get_context_
data(**kwargs)
        ctx["form"] = self.get_form()

        return ctx

    def get_queryset(self):
        form = self.get_form()
        return FormResponse.objects.filter(form=form)

    def get_form(self):
        return FormSchema.objects.get(pk=self.kwargs["form_pk"])
```

Next, create the `main/templates/form_responses.html` template:

```html
{% extends "base.html" %}

{% block content %}
<h1>Responses for {{ form.title }}</h1>
{% if object_list %}
<ul>
    {% for response in object_list %}
    <li>{{ response.response }}</li>
    {% endfor %}
</ul>
{% endif %}
{% endblock %}
```

In `formmason/urls.py`, import our new view:

```python
from main.views import FormResponsesListView
```

Add this URL pattern to the `urlpatterns` list:

```python
url(r'^form/(?P<form_pk>\d+)/responses/$', FormResponsesListView.as_
view(), name='form-responses'),
```

Finally, edit `main/templates/home.html` to add a link to this new view:

```
{% extends "base.html" %}

{% block content %}
    <h1>Available Forms</h1>
    {% if object_list %}
    <ul>
        {% for form in object_list %}
        <li>
            <a href="{% url 'custom-form' form_pk=form.pk %}">{{ form.
title }}</a><br />
            <a href="{% url 'form-responses' form_pk=form.pk %}">See
Responses</a>
        </li>
        {% endfor %}
    </ul>
    {% endif %}
{% endblock %}
```

The new line of code is highlighted. After making all these changes, open the home page and you should see the **See Responses** links for the new view next to each of the existing form links:

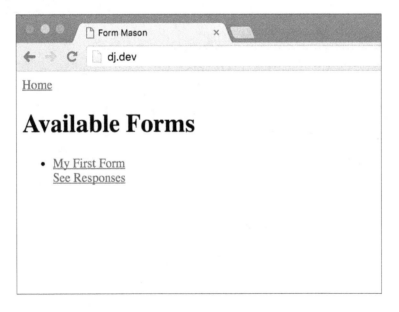

Clicking on the link should take you to a page as follows:

While it does get the job done, it is very crude. We can do better. Let's improve this.

An improved responses list

What we'd like is to show the responses in a tabular fashion with the field names as the header and response values for these fields underneath them. Let's start out by modifying our view code. In main/views.py, first import TemplateView as we will no longer be using ListView as the base class for our FormResponsesListView:

```
from django.views.generic import TemplateView
```

Next, modify FormResponsesListView to match the following code:

```
class FormResponsesListView(TemplateView):
    template_name = "form_responses.html"

    def get_context_data(self, **kwargs):
        ctx = super(FormResponsesListView, self).get_context_
data(**kwargs)

        form = self.get_form()
        schema = form.schema
        form_fields = schema.keys()
        ctx["headers"] = form_fields
        ctx["form"] = form

        responses = self.get_queryset()
        responses_list = list()
        for response in responses:
```

```
                        response_values = list()
                        response_data = response.response

                        for field_name in form_fields:
                            if field_name in response_data:
                                response_values.append(response_data[field_name])
                            else:
                                response_values.append('')
                        responses_list.append(response_values)

                    ctx["object_list"] = responses_list

                    return ctx

                def get_queryset(self):
                    form = self.get_form()
                    return FormResponse.objects.filter(form=form)

                def get_form(self):
                    return FormSchema.objects.get(pk=self.kwargs["form_pk"])
```

The major changes here are in the get_context_data method. We also changed the base class to TemplateView from ListView. Let's look at what we are doing in the get_context_data method.

First, we use the keys method on the JSON form schema, which is saved in the FormSchema model, to create a list of field headers. We pass this to the template in the headers context variable.

The slightly complicated part comes next. We loop over each of the FormResponse objects in our database. For each response object, we then loop over the form field names and get that attribute from the response data. We do this because, in the Django template, there is no way to get a value from a dictionary with a variable key name. We could create a custom template tag; however, that would add unnecessary complexity. Instead, we do the same thing in our view, where it is easier. For each response object, we create a list of values that is in the same order as the field headers. We then add this list of field values to our list of responses. The reason that our data is structured in this way becomes clear when we look at our template.

Finally, we assign the list of responses to the `object_list` template context variable and return the context. Next, let's change the `main/templates/form_responses.html` template to match the following:

```
{% extends "base.html" %}

{% block content %}
<h1>Responses for {{ form.title }}</h1>
{% if object_list %}
<table border="1px">
    <tr>
        {% for field_name in headers %}
        <th>{{ field_name }}</th>
        {% endfor %}
    </tr>
    {% for response in object_list %}
    <tr>
        {% for field_value in response %}
        <td>{{ field_value }}</td>
        {% endfor %}
    </tr>
    {% endfor %}
</table>
{% endif %}
{% endblock %}
```

If you understood how our data was structured in the view, the template should be simple enough to follow. These are all the changes that we need to make for now.

If you open the responses page again, you should now see a neatly aligned table, as shown in the following screenshot:

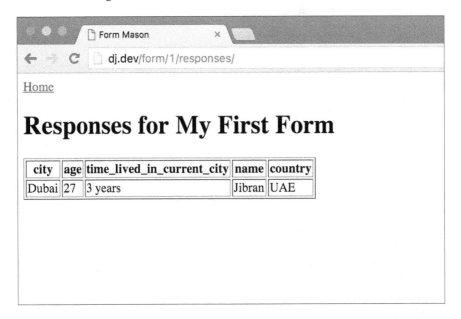

We have so far created a page to list the available forms, a page to submit data with a dynamic form, and a page to show those responses. Our application is nearly done. However, we are still missing a page that allows customers to create a custom form. Let's tackle this next.

Designing a form creation interface

We want to provide our users with a friendly interface to edit the structure of their dynamic forms. The ideal interface would be something that allows users to drag and drop their fields and set the properties for these fields using simple click and type operations on a web page. However, creating an interface like this is a major undertaking and a project on its own. It requires a team of frontend developers and designers to create something that user friendly.

Unfortunately, we can't create something like that as an interface like that is more of a frontend project than something related to Django. However, if you want, it is a good exercise if you are looking to improve your frontend skills.

For this project, we will create a simple Django form where the user can manually enter the JSON to define the structure of their forms. We will provide basic validation and editing capabilities. So let's start by creating our form. Change the `main/forms.py` file to match the following code:

```
import json

from django import forms


class NewDynamicFormForm(forms.Form):
    form_pk = forms.CharField(widget=forms.HiddenInput(),
required=False)
    title = forms.CharField()
    schema = forms.CharField(widget=forms.Textarea())

    def clean_schema(self):
        schema = self.cleaned_data["schema"]
        try:
            schema = json.loads(schema)
        except:
            raise forms.ValidationError("Invalid JSON. Please submit
valid JSON for the schema")

        return schema
```

The form itself is pretty simple. However, we need to take a closer look at the `clean_schema` method. When the `is_valid()` method is called on a Django form, it goes through a couple of steps. The exact details can be found in the documentation at https://docs.djangoproject.com/en/stable/ref/forms/validation/. However, a good approximation is that Django calls two different types of clean methods on the form class. First, it looks for methods named `clean_<fieldname>` for *each* field defined on the form. This method should return the cleaned value of the field that will then be stored in the `cleaned_data` dictionary of the form. Next, Django calls the `clean` method on the form class. This method is meant to clean data for fields that depend on each other as dependent cleaning should not be done in individual `clean_<fieldname>` methods. The `clean` method should return a dictionary that will replace the form's `cleaned_data` dictionary completely.

Either type of clean methods can raise a `forms.ValidationError` exception if the data is not in the expected format. If `ValidationError` is raised in a `clean_<fieldname>` method, the error is tied to that field and displayed next to it when the form is rendered. If the error is raised in the general `clean` method, the error is displayed in the form error list that is displayed right before the form fields start in the HTML of the form.

As we wish to make sure that the data entered by the user in the schema field is valid JSON, we use `json.loads` on the user-entered data and raise an exception if the call fails. One important thing to note is that we return a modified version of the schema if our `clean_schema` call succeeds. This is because, in our model, we need to save a Python dictionary instead of a JSON string. Our `JSONField` model field handles the necessary conversion from a Python object to a JSON string when saving to the database.

Another side note is that the `clean_schema` method is not given any arguments. It must get the value for the schema field from the form's `cleaned_data` dictionary. With our form created, let's add a view to `main/views.py` to display this form. First, import our new form and the `json` library at the top:

```python
import json
from main.forms import NewDynamicFormForm
```

Then add the following code to the view:

```python
class CreateEditFormView(FormView):
    form_class = NewDynamicFormForm
    template_name = "create_edit_form.html"

    def get_initial(self):
        if "form_pk" in self.kwargs:
            form = FormSchema.objects.get(pk=self.kwargs["form_pk"])
            initial = {
                "form_pk": form.pk,
                "title": form.title,
                "schema": json.dumps(form.schema)
            }
        else:
            initial = {}

        return initial

    def get_context_data(self, **kwargs):
        ctx = super(CreateEditFormView, self).get_context_
data(**kwargs)
        if "form_pk" in self.kwargs:
            ctx["form_pk"] = self.kwargs["form_pk"]

        return ctx

    def form_valid(self, form):
```

```
        cleaned_data = form.cleaned_data

        if cleaned_data.get("form_pk"):
            old_form = FormSchema.objects.get(pk=cleaned_data["form_
pk"])
            old_form.title = cleaned_data["title"]
            old_form.schema = cleaned_data["schema"]
            old_form.save()
        else:
            new_form = FormSchema(title=cleaned_data["title"],
schema=cleaned_data["schema"])
            new_form.save()

        return HttpResponseRedirect(reverse("home"))
```

Next, create the `main/templates/create_edit_form.html` file and put this code in there:

```
{% extends "base.html" %}

{% block content %}
<h1>Create/Edit Form</h1>

{% if form_pk %}
<form action="{% url 'edit-form' form_pk=form_pk%}" method="post">{%
csrf_token %}
{% else %}
<form action="{% url 'create-form' %}" method="post">{% csrf_token %}
{% endif %}

{{ form.as_p }}
<input type="submit" value="Create Form" />
</form>
{% endblock %}
```

Finally, import this new view in our `formmason/urls.py` and add two patterns for it to the `urlpatterns` file. Here is the final `formmason/urls.py` file:

```
from django.conf.urls import url

from main.views import CreateEditFormView
from main.views import CustomFormView
from main.views import FormResponsesListView
from main.views import HomePageView

urlpatterns = [
```

```
    url(r'^$', HomePageView.as_view(), name='home'),
    url(r'^form/(?P<form_pk>\d+)/$', CustomFormView.as_view(),
name='custom-form'),
    url(r'^form/(?P<form_pk>\d+)/responses/$', FormResponsesListView.
as_view(), name='form-responses'),

    url(r'form/new/$', CreateEditFormView.as_view(), name='create-
form'),
    url(r'form/(?P<form_pk>\d+)/edit/$', CreateEditFormView.as_view(),
name='edit-form'),
]
```

We are using the same view twice—once as a create view and once as an edit view. If you look at the code for the view, we provide the form with initial data from a FormSchema object if the form_pk keyword argument was matched from the URL. If it wasn't, we know that we are creating a new form and our initial data dictionary is empty. One thing to note is that in the initial data, we use json.dumps(form.schema) to provide the initial value for the schema field. This is the reverse of what we do in the clean_schema method of our form. That's because form.schema is a Python object; however, our frontend needs to show the JSON for the structure. So we convert from a Python object to a JSON string using the json.dumps method.

We handle both the cases—new form creation and form editing—in the form_valid method of our view. On successfully saving or creating our form, we redirect the user to the home page again.

The last thing we need to do is add links to our base template and home page to create and edit forms. First, add this link right after the link for **Home** in templates/base.html:

```
<a href="{% url 'create-form' %}">Create New Form</a>
```

In main/templates/home.html, add this after the link for **See Responses**:

```
<br /><a href="{% url 'edit-form' form_pk=form.pk %}">Edit Form</a>
```

That's it. Let's test it out. Open the home page at `http://127.0.0.1:8000/` first and you should see something similar to the following screenshot:

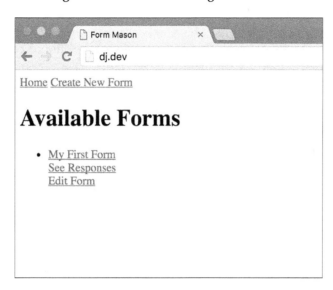

Click on the **Edit Form** button and you should see the following page:

Let's change the title to something new and then type this in the **Schema** field:

```
{"years_of_experience": "number", "occupation": "string"}
```

Click on the **Create New Form** link. This should save the form and take you back to the home page. The title of your form on the home page should be changed to whatever you edited it to. Click on the link to see the form, and you should see a screen similar to this:

Nice! Our form has changed to match the schema that we entered while editing the form. Let's take a look at what our responses page looks like. Submit some test data with the new form schema and open up the responses page. You should see something like this:

This page works as expected, without having to change any of the code. You'll see that the previous responses are no longer visible; however, there seems to be some empty cells above the latest response. We'll look into fixing this and other small issues next. However, our application is complete except for a few small fixes that we need to do.

You should use the **Create New Form** link at the top of the pages as well to create a new form and test it out. It should work as expected.

Small fixes

I noticed three small errors while working on this last section that I'd like to fix. First of all, if you take a closer look at the form submission page (where the user can enter data in a custom form), you'll notice that the heading on the top says **Custom Form**. This is from our first test, when our form schema was defined in a hardcoded JSON string and didn't have a title. As our form model now has a title field, edit `main/templates/custom_form.html` and change the `h1` tag to match the following:

```
<h1>{{ form_schema.title }}</h1>
```

Next, edit `CustomFormView` in `main/views.py` and add the `this get_context_data` method to the class:

```
def get_context_data(self, **kwargs):
    ctx = super(CustomFormView, self).get_context_data(**kwargs)

    form_schema = FormSchema.objects.get(pk=self.kwargs["form_pk"])
    ctx["form_schema"] = form_schema

    return ctx
```

Look at the form detail page again. This time, the heading should reflect the form title, as shown in the following screenshot:

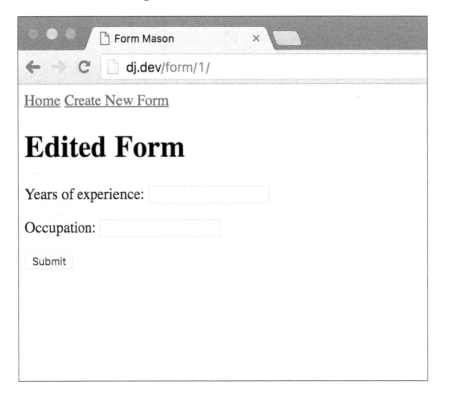

The next error that I noticed was on the form editing page. Right now, whether you are creating a new form or editing an existing one, the heading always says `Create/Edit Form` and the **Submit** button always says **Create New Form**. Let's modify our `main/templates/create_edit_form.html` template to tell the user explicitly what action they are taking. Here is the final code for the template:

```
{% extends "base.html" %}

{% block content %}
{% if form_pk %}
    <h1>Edit Form</h1>
{% else %}
    <h1>Create Form</h1>
{% endif %}

{% if form_pk %}
<form action="{% url 'edit-form' form_pk=form_pk%}" method="post">{%
csrf_token %}
{% else %}
<form action="{% url 'create-form' %}" method="post">{% csrf_token %}
{% endif %}
    {{ form.as_p }}
    {% if form_pk %}
        <input type="submit" value="Save Form" />
    {% else %}
        <input type="submit" value="Create Form" />
    {% endif %}
</form>
{% endblock %}
```

Now if you edit an existing form or create a new one, the heading and button should match that action:

The last issue I saw was on the responses page. If you edit a form that already has responses and the new form has none of the fields that the old form had, you will see some empty table rows at the start. That's because even though our view code doesn't include any data for those rows, it still includes an empty row. Let's fix this by modifying the `get_context_data` method of `FormResponsesListView` in `main/views.py`. Look for this piece of code:

```
for field_name in form_fields:
    if field_name in response_data:
```

```
            response_values.append(response_data[field_name])
        else:
            response_values.append('')
    responses_list.append(response_values)
```

Change it to the following:

```
for field_name in form_fields:
    if field_name in response_data:
        response_values.append(response_data[field_name])
    else:
        response_values.append('')
if any(response_values):
    responses_list.append(response_values)
```

The last two lines, the highlighted ones, are the changes. The `any` function is a built-in Python method that returns `True` if any of the values in the given list evaluates to `True`. If our `responses_list` contains all empty strings, which is the case if our new form structure has no fields that overlap with the old form structure, the `if` condition will fail and we will not include a completely empty row in our responses list. Try looking at the responses list page again and you should see that the empty rows have now disappeared:

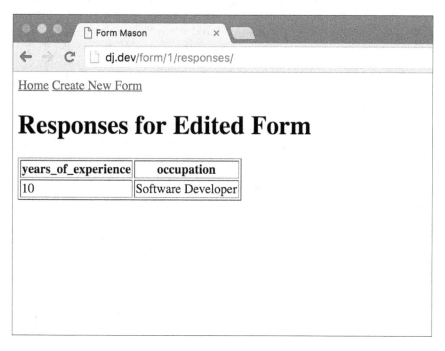

That's it. Our last, and most ambitious, application is complete. Congratulations! You have come a long way from the simple blog that we created at the start of this book. You should now be ready to tackle any web application project that comes your way.

Summary

This chapter was more about exploration than new concepts. The only major new concept that you learned was about the inner workings of Django forms, and this section took up fewer than five pages. The rest of the chapter was about finding solutions to problems that we encountered along the way.

As I said at the start of this chapter, this was the most complicated application that we have created in the book. It is also likely to be one of the more complicated applications you will create at the start of your career. It is by no means a polished product; that's more because we didn't do any frontend work, rather than some lack of features in the Django backend.

While the knowledge we gained about Django forms in this chapter will prove invaluable to you, I would like the main takeaway from it to be the approach to solving problems. We found a problem we needed to solve, we experimented in the Django shell, and we found a solution. Sometimes it's a bit more complicated than that. You probably need to search the Internet for existing solutions or ask your colleagues. However, after finding answers that seem to be relevant to your problem, you will always have to go back to the experimentation and make sure that the solution really does solve your problem.

The way I showed you how to play around in the Django shell is just one of the many ways that you can choose to experiment with different solutions. As I've mentioned before, everyone has their own technique. Some use management commands, some use simple Python scripts, and some write test code in the views. In the end, you will come up with a way that you like the best.

Another thing that I hope you take away from this chapter is the use of external libraries to help solve our problems. When we needed a way to store JSON in our database, we used the `jsonfield` library that was available as open source instead of rolling our own custom solution. This has benefits and drawbacks. The benefits are that if you find a package, such as `jsonfield` that is widely used, you will get a solution that has been tested by many before you. Due to that testing, the library will be much more stable than what you, or any person, can come up with on your own. The drawback of using something external is that you have no control over the direction the project takes and in some projects, you'll have to painstakingly go over the code for the external library to make sure that it meets any regulations your project might have about external code usage.

However, personally, I prefer to use a tried and tested third-party library every time over creating something by myself. For me, the pros usually outweigh the cons.

That's it! This was the final chapter in this epic journey that we started with a simple blog! We have come a long way from where we started; however, I'm sure that your journey as a Django web developer is just starting. You have many more exciting things to look forward to, and I wish you the best of luck in this journey. I hope you enjoyed reading this book as much as I enjoyed writing it. Bon voyage!

Development Environment Setup Details and Debugging Techniques

This appendix will go into further detail about the Django development environment setup that we have been using throughout the book. We will look into the details of the setup, and I will explain each of the steps that we took. I will also show you a technique for debugging Django applications. For this appendix, we will assume that the project we are setting up is the Blueblog project from the first chapter.

We will start our project by first creating a root directory for it and then cd into the directory so that all our commands are run inside it:

```
> mkdir blueblog
> cd blueblog
```

There is no technical reason for this. I just prefer to keep all the files related to a project in one directory as it makes things easier to organize when you have to add further files related to a project, such as designs and other documentation.

Next, we will create a virtual environment to use for the project. Virtual environments are a feature that allow you to create lightweight installations of Python so that each of your projects can have its own installation of all the libraries that it uses. This is useful when you are working on multiple projects at the same time and each project requires a separate version of some library. For example, at work, I once had to work on two projects at the same time. One required Django 1.4; the other required Django 1.9. If I hadn't used virtual environments, it would have been very difficult to keep both versions of Django at the same time.

Virtual environments also allow you to keep your Python environment clean, which is very important when you are finally ready to deploy your application to a production server. When deploying your application to a server, you need to be able to accurately reproduce the same Python environment you had in your development machine. If you don't use a separate virtual environment for each project, you will need to figure out exactly which Python libraries your project uses and then only install those on the production server. With a virtual environment, you no longer need to spend time figuring out which of the installed Python libraries are related to your project. You can just create a list of all the libraries installed in the virtual environment and install them on the production server, confident that you won't miss out on anything or install anything extra that you don't use.

If you want to read more about virtual environments, you can read the official documentation at `https://docs.python.org/3/library/venv.html`.

To create the virtual environment, we use the `pyvenv` command:

```
> pyvenv blueblogEnv
```

This creates a new environment inside the `blueblogEnv` folder. Once we have created the environment, we activate it:

```
> source blueblogEnv/bin/activate
```

Activating the environment makes sure that any Python commands we run or any libraries we install will use the activated environment. Next, we install Django in our new environment and start our project:

```
> pip install django
> django-admin.py startproject blueblog src
```

This creates a directory called `src` that holds our Django project. You can name the directory anything you want; this is just the convention I prefer.

And that's all there is to the setup of our development environment.

Using pdb to debug Django views

You will often come across problems in your Django applications that are not immediately clear. When I get stuck with a tough bug, especially when it's inside a Django view, I use the Python debugger, which is built into Python, to step through my view code and debug the problem. To do so, you'll need to put this line of code into your view right before the point where you think the problem exists:

```
import pdb; pdb.set_trace()
```

Then, the next time you load the page associated with that view, you'll see that your browser appears to not load anything. This is because your Django application is now paused. If you look in the console where you ran the `runserver` command, you should see a prompt for `pdb`. In the prompt, you can type the name of any variable available in the current Python scope (usually the scope of the view that you are debugging) and it will print the current value of that variable. You can also run a bunch of other debugging commands. For a complete list of available features, take a look at the documentation for the Python debugger at `https://docs.python.org/3/library/pdb.html`.

A good Stack Overflow question with useful answers that lists some other debugging techniques is `http://stackoverflow.com/questions/1118183/how-to-debug-in-django-the-good-way`.

Developing on Windows

If you are going to be using the Windows operating system while reading this book, please note that a couple of things will need to be done differently. Firstly, all the instructions provided in this book assume a Linux/Mac OS X environment, and some commands may not work as is. The most important change is how Windows handles file paths. On a Linux/OS X environment, paths are written with a forward slash. All the paths mentioned in the book are formatted similarly, for example, `PROJECT_DIR/main/settings.py`. When referring to these paths on Windows, you will need to change the forward slashes to backslashes. This path will become `PROJECT_DIR\main\settings.py`.

Secondly, while Python is normally included with or easily installed on Linux/OS X, you will need to follow the instructions at `https://www.python.org/downloads/windows/` to install it on Windows. After you have Python installed, you can install Django using the instructions at `https://docs.djangoproject.com/en/stable/howto/windows/`.

There are a few other things that will need to be modified for Windows. I have mentioned these in the book as they have come up, but I might have missed something. If so, a search on Google will usually lead you to an answer. If not, you can always look me up on Twitter at `@theonejb` and I'll do my best to help you.

Index

F

fake data, Djagios
generating 77
management commands, using 77-80
model representation 81
FileField model field 114, 115
file uploads
reference link 115
fixtures
about 112
URL 114
used, for loading data 113, 114
for loops
reference link 88
Form Mason
code pack 200
Django form, creating 200-202
dynamic forms, generating 203, 204
errors, handling 231-236
field, adding to SampleForm instance 203
form creation interface, designing 224-231
model, creating 209-212
responses, displaying 219-221
responses, improving 221-224
responses, saving 217, 218
user interface, creating 213-217
form validation
reference link 225
form_valid method
URL 42

G

generic views
URL 9
get_absolute_url method
URL 116
using 116

I

ImageField model field 114, 115
internationalization (i18n) 133
Internet Movie Database (IMDB) 133
ipython 201

J

JavaScript Object Notation (JSON)
about 203
benefits 204
used, for generating dynamic
forms 205-209
json module
URL 205

L

l10n 133
language preferences, Django
reference link 143
lite search 163
localization 133
login/logout, BlueBlog
handling 10, 11
login view, defining 11, 12
logout view, defining 12, 13
navigation links, adding 13
login_required decorator
URL 19
login view
URL 12

M

Machine to machine (M2M) 61
management commands
about 77
URL 79
using 77-80
mapping
about 165, 166
defining 167, 168
META dictionary
URL 103
method_decorator
URL 19
modeltranslation library
reference link 149
Multilingual Movie Database (MMDB)
about 133
code pack 134

www.ingramcontent.com/pod-product-compliance
Lightning Source LLC
LaVergne TN
LVHW081339050326
832903LV00024B/1205